**Some of the conversations
you'll hear in . . .**

# BOYFRIENDS

"I feel like my whole life is changing. I swing back and forth from a joyful feeling to a fear that he may not love me any more."

MARVA, 18

"I want to do lots of different things with the girl I go out with. If all she wants to do is sit around and mope, I'll quickly get bored with her. When we're together we should have fun and enjoy each other's company."

DAVID, 14

"I'd change the color of my eyes. Plain brown is so ugly. If you're not pretty, most guys won't give you the time of day."

ARIEL, 14

"What attracts me most is how intelligent she is and what kind of personality she has. If I went for looks alone, I might end up with a girl who had the I.Q. of a steak."

MICHAEL, 16

*Also by Joyce Vedral:*

I DARE YOU*
MY PARENTS ARE DRIVING ME CRAZY*
I CAN'T TAKE IT ANYMORE*
THE OPPOSITE SEX IS DRIVING ME CRAZY*
MY TEENAGER IS DRIVING ME CRAZY*

*Physical Fitness Titles:*

NOW OR NEVER
SUPER CUT
HARD BODIES
PERFECT PARTS
THE HARD BODIES EXPRESS WORKOUT
THE 12-MINUTE TOTAL-BODY WORKOUT

*Published by Ballantine Books

# BOYFRIENDS

*Getting Them, Keeping Them,*
*Living Without Them*

# Joyce L. Vedral, Ph.D.

BALLANTINE BOOKS • NEW YORK

# Dedication

To you, the young ladies of the nineties, who are reaching for your highest star and who will not allow anything, even boyfriends, to hold you back.

# Contents

# Acknowledgments

To Marthe Simone Vedral, for your insightful reading of the manuscript and for your many contributions to the text.

To the students of Julia Richman High School in New York City and of General Douglas McArthur High School in Wantagh, Long Island, for your colorful interviews.

To teenagers from all over the United States, for allowing me to interview you for this book.

To Bob Wyatt, Editor-in-Chief, for remaining a teenager at heart. You are a delightful, rare gem.

To my agent, Rick Balkin, for your vision concerning this project.

To Richard McCoy, for your endless patience in working out the details for this project.

To all of the "boyfriends" and young men of the world, both those who have caused pain and those who have caused joy, for providing insight through which we can grow.

To family and friends, for your continual support.

To Dr. Dorothy Sacknoff, for your wisdom and sensitivity concerning matters of the heart. I learned a lot from you.

# 1

# There's Always *Someone* Better Looking than You, So . . .

The truth is, if looks were the most important quality needed to attract and keep a boyfriend, we would all be in serious trouble—because the moment a better-looking girl came along, we would lose our boyfriend. What a nightmare. Can you imagine the pressure? And just think about what would happen on days when our hair, makeup, or clothing was a little off. Off would go our boyfriend, too.

I almost named this chapter "How to Get a Guy Away from a Girl Who's Prettier than You," because that's exactly what you'll know how to do by the time you finish reading this book. But by then you won't be worrying about looks so much because you'll realize that the much-repeated saying "Looks aren't everything" is really true.

Why do most teenage girls suffer from "looks insecurity"? What do teenage boys look for in girls if it's not just their physical beauty? And, surprisingly, why do guys often leave the prettiest girl standing alone and talk to the beauty queen's friends?

In this chapter you'll find out the answers to these questions. But as you read the rest of this book, you'll find out more. You'll learn how you can meet and talk to the guy you're most attracted to and how to get him to fall in love with you. You'll find out how to tell if you're really in love and how to let a guy down gently when you've fallen out of love with him. You'll discover how to keep your friends when you're tempted to drop them all and spend most of your time with your boyfriend, and you'll find out why relationships change so much once sex enters the picture. You'll learn how to keep a guy guessing so that he doesn't take you for granted and how to handle cheating.

Perhaps most important, however, you'll learn to find the inner strength to let go of a relationship that is destructive to you, even if you're still in love with the guy, and you'll learn that as a matter of fact, you don't need a boyfriend in order to enjoy life.

Yes. By the time you've turned the last page of this book, you'll understand that a boyfriend can be a wonderful addition to your life, but that you don't really need one to be happy. You'll never again feel that if you break up with your boyfriend life is not worth living. In other words, you'll learn how to keep a part of yourself separate from your boyfriend, no matter how madly or passionately in love you are, so that if you do break up, as your boyfriend is walking out the door, you won't feel as if your entire reason for living is going with him. All of these things and more will be discussed in this book, so that once and for all you can enjoy your life with or without a boyfriend. But now, back to . . .

## LOOKS ANXIETY

Most girls are unhappy with at least one aspect of their looks. I asked teenage girls, if they could magically change one thing about themselves so that guys would be more attracted to them, what it would be. They said:

My hair. It just won't grow long. If I could get hair extensions, my problems would be solved.

*Deidre, 16*

2

I have thin, stringy, ugly long hair. I would give anything for a thick head of hair.

*Kathy, 13*

I hate the color of my hair. It's mousy brown. People tell me, "But it's so thick and shiny," but everyone knows blondes have more fun.

*Sandra, 16*

I'm a blonde but blondes are a dime a dozen. Black hair is so much more dramatic. I wish my parents would let me dye my hair.

*Jeanie, 15*

My long nose. It's a beak. Guys my age are interested in stereotyped perfect looks. If you don't have them, you're out.

*Kay, 15*

My pug nose looks like a pig's nose—so short and turned up. No guy likes to look at a girl with a pig's nose.

*Camille, 17*

I'd change the color of my eyes. Plain brown is so ugly. If you're not pretty, most guys won't give you the time of day.

*Ariel, 14*

My eyes are this washed-out blue. I would make them bluer.

*Nancy, 18*

I'm too tall, and guys who are shorter than me go for the short girls.

*Cassandra, 16*

I'm only five feet and they call me "shrimpboat." Short girls are just not sexy. You can't even enter a beauty contest if you're short.

*Laurie, 15*

If I had bigger hips I'd be so much sexier.

*Alice, 15*

If I could lose this big butt and my huge hips I wouldn't look like a hog. I'm not fat, but I'm "hefty," and I hate it.

*Connie, 16*

I wear a size-nine shoe, and all guys see when they come up to me are my monster feet.

*Nadine, 15*

These braces drive all the guys away. I stopped smiling ever since I got them, but that doesn't help.

*Lillian, 13*

I'm too flat-chested. Don't tell me I wouldn't get more guys if I wore a size 36D.

*Edith, 17*

I have to keep on top of the zits at all times, and no matter how much cover-up I use, they show through. I picture all the guys staring at my ugly face and saying, No way am I going to kiss that.

*Jody, 16*

Hair, nose, eyes, height, weight, shape, teeth, feet, breasts, complexion—you name it. Brunettes want to be blondes and blondes want to be brunettes. Girls with short hair want long hair and girls with long hair want thicker hair. Girls with long noses want smaller noses, but girls with pug noses call their noses snouts. Brown-eyed girls want blue eyes, but blue-eyed girls are not satisfied with the shade of blue. Tall girls want to be short, but short girls want to be tall. Thin girls want bigger hips, but more curvaceous girls want straighter hips.

Where does it end? The fact is, no girl is ever completely satisfied with her looks. Girls falsely believe: "If only I could change this about me, I could get the guy of my dreams." But you don't have to change a single thing to get to meet the guy you have in mind, because guys are looking at much more than that "fault" when they see you. They look at the whole picture, or what is known as the "gestalt." That picture includes your looks, your energy, the way you carry yourself, and your personality.

Contrary to your fears, there is no spotlight on the long nose, the brown hair, the zit, or the big feet. The fault that is so magnified in your eyes is instead incorporated into an entire picture when a guy looks at you. You'll realize this is true if you think about how you look at guys. A guy can have freckles or big ears or be a little short, but if other things are great, you quickly forgive the "fault." In fact, you may be so charmed by his fetching smile, the twinkle in his eye, the way he laughs, or the stories he tells, that you completely forget the physical defect. I'll bet you can think of a guy right now who looks completely different to you from the way he appeared when you first met him, because the attractiveness of his personality has not only made up for his flaws, but has transformed them. Beauty really is in the eye of the beholder.

That may be one reason why people are not evenly matched when it comes to looks. Isn't it true that you've often seen a very handsome guy with a not-so-pretty girl? The reverse is also true. You'll find stunning women with not-so-good-looking men—guys with acne going out with girls who have satin-smooth skin and so on. Why is this so? It's obvious that people are attracted to each other for something more than just looks.

Let's find out what the something more is.

## WHAT ATTRACTS A GUY TO A GIRL?

I asked teenage guys to tell exactly what it is that attracts them to a girl and makes them want to ask her out, even if she has far from perfect looks. Here's what they said:

What makes a girl pretty to me is the way she carries herself. If she has a positive attitude, that means everything.

*Randy, 17*

It's the sparkle in her eyes, the sound of her voice, the words she says.

*Victor, 15*

I'm attracted to soft-spoken girls—girls who are humble and not stuck-up, and who are open enough to talk to you.

*Ryan, 14*

I can tell by a girl's face if she's a happy person (not grumpy or stupid). If she's nice and friendly, then those traits make her the prettiest in the world.

*David, 18*

I'm attracted by a girl's warmth and the way she responds to me. In my mind, beauty is the total of all of her characteristics. That's why a girl looks pretty to me sometimes, even if others don't see it.

*Chris, 19*

If a girl was in a group, say at school, I could tell more about her. If she's down to earth and fun to be with, I'll be attracted to her.

*Scott, 16*

Nobody is perfect. If a girl has high spirits and can keep me in high spirits, too, what a treasure she is.

*Caesar, 18*

What attracts me most is how intelligent she is and what kind of personality she has. If I went for looks alone, I might end up with a girl who had the I.Q. of a steak.

*Michael, 16*

I found out that after I spend time with a girl, she either gets prettier or uglier. It has nothing to do with her real looks. It's her personality.

*Joe, 17*

I'm attracted to a girl by the way she conducts herself. Later her inner feelings and her self-esteem make me more attracted to her.

*Eddie, 19*

A positive attitude, friendliness and warmth, joy, high spirits, self-confidence, and a sparkle in the eye are all reflections of inner qualities. They make the external qualities or the looks become beautiful. It seems clear to me that guys are saying that personality is more important than looks.

But what is a "personality" anyway? It's the person behind the face and body. The real person, after all, is not the façade presented to the world, but the energy that comes from within. You can see this clearly if you've ever been to the funeral of someone you loved. You look in the casket, and no matter how good a job the mortician has done on the body, the person you loved is obviously not there. All that is left is an empty shell. What is missing? The self or the soul, or as I've been calling it, the personality.

Another way to understand the importance of personality is to imagine the effect of a personality transplant. For example, think of your favorite teacher, the one with the sense of humor and the good nature, and think of your most dreaded teacher, the one who is mean and rigid. Imagine the mean teacher walking into class with the other teacher's personality. Wouldn't that teacher's very appearance seem to alter after a while? Wouldn't the mean teacher actually start to look better once a different personality was behind those hated features? So you see, personality is more important than looks. And I think that's great news, because it's easier to alter our personality than our looks—and it doesn't even require plastic surgery.

## PERSONALITY TRAITS GUYS LOVE

What personality traits are most likely to attract guys? Although you might think they would talk a lot about sexiness, not one of the guys mentioned that specifically. Obviously, what makes a girl sexy is a combination of other traits. Here's what the guys had to say:

A girl with a sense of humor is best. She's not so self-conscious and she's not all uptight. I love that.

*Billy, 15*

7

If she's friendly to my friends and fun to be with, then I could fall in love with her.

*Tony, 14*

I like a sweet, sensitive girl.

*Mark, 17*

I like a girl with a goal, one who isn't lazy.

*Tom, 16*

She should have an intelligent attitude and be interested in self-improvement. Also, I love when a girl can carry on a conversation.

*Lou, 18*

I like independence and generosity.

*Andy, 15*

I like a girl who's understanding and caring, someone I can relate to as a friend and who I can talk to about anything.

*Les, 15*

Interesting. Guys seem to like personality traits that put them at ease. A sense of humor, friendliness, and warmth tell a guy that he won't be judged harshly by that girl, and he gets the message that he can relax and be himself.

In addition, guys respect girls who show independence and drive. Girls who have a goal in life are exciting to guys. They carry with them a sense of adventure. It seems clear, then, that concentrating on changing your looks is a waste of time. What you need to do is to relax and be yourself. If you let the real you shine through—your sense of humor, your wit, your sensitivity, your compassion, yes, everything that is best about you—you'll find more and more guys beginning to talk to you. Of course, not every guy will fall in love with you, but don't worry. The ones who are suited to you will. Anyway, it's just as well that those who are not suited to you find out and go their way. Why waste your time on a guy who doesn't like the real you? There will be plenty of others who do. Really!

## BEAUTIFUL GIRLS HAVE TROUBLES TOO

The fact is, girls with striking beauty often have more trouble meeting guys than middle-of-the-road lookers. Why? Because many guys are intimidated by really good-looking girls. They won't even approach such girls because they fear being rejected, and they assume the competition will be too stiff for them. You don't believe me? Let's see what the guys say. I asked them whether or not they would approach the prettiest girl in a group. They said:

No, because most of them act like they're "it." In my experience, if she's great-looking she may not want to talk to me, so I would avoid her.

*Jack, 15*

The prettiest one usually has the worst attitude. I don't need a girl who's thinking only of herself. I need one who will think of me a little.

*Joe, 18*

If I think she's the prettiest in the group, someone else does, too. Why should I try?

*Sam, 16*

The prettiest girl may think she can play me for a fool.
*Herbert, 18*

No, man. If she's that pretty, you know she's got a boyfriend, so why bother?

*Jason, 14*

No. She might think she's too good for me. Like Miss America or something.

*Anthony, 14*

9

See what I mean? Discrimination if I've ever heard of it. Prejudice, plain and simple. A pretty girl really has to pass a lot of tests before a guy will give her a chance—and that is assuming he's even willing to talk to her. Most guys, as you can see, won't give her that much of a chance. They assume that just because a girl is pretty, she thinks she's God's gift to the world, and they don't dare to take a chance at being rejected by her. As a matter of fact, I've had to counsel pretty girls on how to make a guy feel at ease by smiling, starting a conversation, and giving a guy a compliment. It's actually the prettiest girls who have the hardest time meeting the guys they're interested in—unless they learn to make the first move. But pretty or not so pretty, you'll learn what to do to meet a guy you're attracted to, and it will work. More of that in the next chapter.

In the meantime, let's face it, no matter what we look like, we can either sit around feeling sorry for ourselves and waste our energy being jealous of others, or we can make the most of what we have. The latter's a lot more fun, and a great adventure as well. You just never know what's going to happen when you start using your brain and begin taking chances. Once you dare to be yourself, anything can happen. It's exciting. Read on and let the fun begin.

## REMINDERS

1. No teenage girl is completely satisfied with her looks. Most girls would change one or more features if they could, in the false belief that this change would make them more popular with guys.
2. The simple truth is, guys are intimidated by gorgeous girls, and it's the prettiest girls who often have the most trouble meeting guys.
3. Guys are looking for a lot more than a face and a figure. They are searching for girls who are warm, charming, witty, adventurous, and friendly—girls who make them feel good about themselves. Therefore guys often fall in love with girls who are not as good-looking as they are.

10

4. Your personality is the *you* behind your looks (your façade). It's your personality that shines through and causes you to appear either better-looking or worse-looking.
5. Once you dare to allow your unique personality to shine through, you'll start attracting guys you never thought you could get. It's no mystery. People are looking for "soulmates."

# 2

# How to Meet the Guy You Have Your Eye On

Forget the old saying "You can't find love and romance when you're looking for it." In fact, the opposite is true. It's when you're looking that you're most likely to find it. All you have to do is . . . well, that's what this chapter is all about.

Something I see all the time frustrates me. Girl likes boy, and boy likes girl—yet boy refuses to talk to girl because boy thinks he may be rejected, and girl refuses to approach boy because girl assumes boy doesn't like her (otherwise why wouldn't he make the first move?). So although boy and girl like each other and would love to meet each other, they never do. This very situation occurred recently with my sixteen-year-old daughter, Marthe—but fortunately, her story has a happy ending.

Marthe had broken up with her boyfriend some time ago, and it seemed to her that she was the only girl in her school without a boyfriend. While that wasn't the case, it *was* true that all of her close friends had boyfriends. Because her friends were usually occupied with their boyfriends on the weekends and she had no one to go out with to meet new guys, she wondered how she would ever meet anyone.

Then one day she came home from school with a strange

smile on her face. When I asked her what was up, she said: "There's this really hot new guy in school, but I think he has a girlfriend." "How do you know that?" I asked. She said: "He's so good-looking, of course he has a girlfriend." A few days passed and Marthe seemed depressed. "It's no use," she said. "That guy just keeps to himself every day. He stands alone by the wall in the cafeteria, not talking to anyone. I don't have a chance, and these girls pick him up after school." "Why don't you go up and talk to him?" I asked. (I knew I was asking for something big because Marthe is not the type to do that. She's a bit shy.) "Right. Sure. I'm going to go right up to him and say, 'Hi. My name is Marthe. What's your name?' " "Okay, so you don't have to do that, just get his attention and give him a big Hollywood smile, and when he sees you, just keep on looking at him and smiling."

The next day Marthe came home happy. "I did it and it worked," she said. "He smiled back, and later when I saw him in the hall, he waved to me." Before you know it, they were talking and, at this moment, they're going out. In fact, you can't pry them apart.

In this chapter you'll find out how to meet the guy *you* have your eye on. There will be many suggestions, and not all of them will be ones you'll want to try out—at least not immediately. But one or two will strike you as things you would feel comfortable doing, and once you see how well they work, you may be willing to attempt some of the others. Before you know it, you'll be meeting boys with no trouble at all. In addition, you'll find out, perhaps to your surprise, that guys love it when girls "break the ice." It's a great relief to them and it's *always* a welcome compliment—regardless of whether it leads to anything.

## SMILE, SMILE, SMILE

Let's start with the easiest thing—smiling. Everyone loves a smile. A smile sends a message to the person you smile at. "I am friendly and good-hearted," it says. "I will not reject

13

you or 'dis' you (disrespect you) if you speak to me. I would like to get to know you. You seem interesting to me.'' It gives a guy courage—and believe me, he needs it. Guys are even more afraid of rejection than girls are—as you'll see when you read what they say about how they feel when a girl smiles at them.

I like the girl immediately. It makes me feel good because it means that she finds me attractive and she may like me.

*Andrew, 14*

I get a warm feeling deep down in my gut, because I think she's trying to be friendly—and it tells me that she may think I'm good-looking.

*Leonard, 18*

It tells me she may want to meet me. That's how conversations start. It gives me the feeling that it's okay to go up and talk to her.

*Bill, 17*

I'm the kind of guy that keeps to himself. I'm a little shy, in a way. If a girl smiles at me, it makes me take notice of the girl in the first place. Then I might talk to her.

*Joseph, 18*

It's great because everyone likes the feeling of being noticed. I feel like I've still got what it takes.

*Milton, 16*

Most of the guys take a smile as a sign that the girl thinks they're attractive, and this gives them the courage to go over and begin a conversation. Without that kind of encouragement, many guys, even the best-looking ones, are too insecure to approach a girl. Maybe she'll laugh or be cruel, or maybe she'll just be indifferent, they worry. A well-timed smile, however, removes this fear. If you're not a smiler, chances are you've missed out on guys who couldn't work up the nerve to talk to you, or didn't notice how attractive you are. An example of this is found in my book, *I Dare You,* only the girl changed the outcome by smiling. Here's what Maria says:

I used to go to the supermarket every week for my mother. All the time I would notice this good-looking guy at the meat counter. So I thought about what you said about the way people have to talk to you if you smile and I said to myself, "Why not give it a try?" So I went over to the meat counter and I waited for him to come out. Then I looked right in his face and smiled at him. He said: "May I help you?" Then he started asking me if I do the family shopping, where I hang out and what school I go to. Before you know it he asked me if I was busy Friday night. I was so excited about this, I got all tongue tied. Anyway, I gave him my phone number and we went out Friday night. (p. 54)

Maria had been seeing the guy for weeks, but nothing happened. And chances are, nothing ever would have happened with that particular guy if she hadn't dared to smile. All those weeks he might have been wishing he could get to know her but feeling too scared to make the first move. Or maybe he never even noticed her until she smiled. In any case, by smiling, Maria got things started.

So smile away. After all, what have you got to lose? What's the worst thing that could happen? He doesn't smile back? Or he does but he turns out to be a real jerk once he starts talking to you? So what? You don't have to marry him. You just politely excuse yourself and walk away. At least now you know you didn't miss out on the love of your life—and more important, you'll respect yourself for having made an effort to take matters into your own hands. You will realize that you don't have to wait for things to happen—that *you* can make them happen if you want to.

What stops you from smiling? You don't know how to smile? You don't feel like smiling? You wear braces? So what? Practice smiling in the mirror if you have to. If you don't feel like smiling, think of something pleasant enough to make you smile. And if you wear braces, smile anyway. A sour face with braces is less likely to get attention than a happy face with braces. Everyone loves a smile.

## WHAT IF YOU SMILE AT A GUY WHO'S NOT ATTRACTED TO YOU?

Of course, there's another reason girls hesitate to smile at guys they're attracted to. They're afraid of rejection. They reason, "If he doesn't think I'm pretty, he may laugh at me or say, 'What are you grinning at, you beast?' "

Well, girls, your fears are in vain. As it turns out, guys are a lot more sensitive and gentle than you may have realized. Perhaps this is because a guy knows how much it hurts when he likes a girl who's not attracted to him and she makes fun of him or says something cruel. I asked guys: If a girl you're not attracted to smiled at you, what would you do?

I wouldn't mind. I'd just think she's being friendly. I'd still be happy because I'd realize that even girls I'm not attracted to are attracted to me.

*Michael, 16*

I would just smile back and be pleasant. I am happy to get the attention.

*Shamal, 17*

I'd think maybe she likes me a little bit. So I'd smile back because I wouldn't want to hurt her feelings or make her feel unwanted, but I wouldn't make it anything more than that.

*Ray, 17*

It still makes me feel good because even if I'm not attracted to a girl I can still like her as a friend. I would just give a friendly "Hi" and keep going.

*Bill, 15*

I would smile back and just try not to converse with her.

*George, 18*

I really don't think anything of it. If she wants to have a conversation, I do, because I wouldn't insult anyone.

*Val, 17*

I'd become attracted to her.

*Pete, 18*

It seems to me these guys will take the attention and appreciate it—whether or not they're attracted to the girl. They would feel flattered and smile back out of respect. Some of them would keep on moving after returning the smile, in which case no harm done. But others would start a conversation and hope to make a friend. When this happens, however, there's always the possibility that the friendship could become something more, once the two people get to know each other. Pete, however, doesn't even need to get to know the girl. The smile alone, he says, would make him attracted to her.

You see, ladies, you've nothing to lose and everything to gain. Of course you don't know whether or not a guy finds you attractive, so when you smile, you can't be sure what the end result will be. Maybe you'll hook him, maybe you won't. But either way, if you smile, at least *something* can happen. And if you read the preceding quotations from guys, you know that the worst that can happen is he'll smile back but keep going. Is that so terrible?

## DO GUYS LIKE IT WHEN A GIRL INITIATES A CONVERSATION?

While it's true that no one is stopping a girl from going up to a guy and starting a conversation, it is not considered her obligation to do so. It's an option. Not so in the case of a guy. Traditionally, it is the role of the male to "make the approach." Can you imagine the pressure a guy must feel when he sees a girl he would like to speak to? He knows that he must say something, otherwise he will consider himself a wimp. Yet if he does, he fears he will be rejected. Every time a guy sees a girl he's attracted to, he goes through a battle in his mind. Should I or shouldn't I? And because most teenage guys are very unsure of whether or not they "measure up," no matter how good-looking they are or "macho" they appear, they agonize over the decision. For this reason, when a girl starts the conversation, she does the guy a great favor. No wonder he's likely to appreciate it so much, as all the boys I spoke to did. Here's what they had to say:

If a girl sees a guy she likes and he's just standing there, and nothing happens, she should take the cue and start the conversation. I may be a little shy, so if she starts it, it helps a lot.

*Ron, 16*

I hate to start conversations because I don't know what to say. I hardly ever start talking to a girl first. Lots of times I want to but I'm scared. I like it when a girl starts. It saves me.

*Antoine, 18*

I like it when a girl starts because it shows me that she is open, and it takes a lot of courage.

*Tim, 16*

I like a girl to start because it means she's intelligent, and I'm not bold enough to start.

*Mickey, 17*

It's easier for me if the girl starts talking first because then I know she has an interest in me and I don't have to worry about rejection. If she starts, you have a better chance of going out with her because chances are, she likes you in the first place.

*Steve, 16*

They need your help, girls. They're a lot more afraid of girls than they let on. Often they don't know what to say—and can't think of an opening line. When the girl starts first, it takes the pressure off them. Guys also respect girls who start conversations, because, as Tim and Mickey say, it takes courage.

In addition, they take it as a signal that this girl may be willing to go out with them, and it gives them courage to take the next step and ask for her telephone number or a date.

## HOW GIRLS START CONVERSATIONS

All well and good. But what are some ways to start conversations with guys? Here's what girls say about techniques that have worked for them:

I smile and ask him for the time, or say "What's your name?" You know, just flirt a little.

*Marthe, 16*

I talk about something we have in common. Like if we're standing around school, I'll say, "I can't believe I have a math test."

*Joanne, 15*

I'll make a comment about the hot day or the rainy day or the cold day—whatever. It doesn't matter. They usually pick up on it and take it from there.

*Shanna, 15*

I say, "Haven't I seen you before?" Or you can just walk up and say, "Excuse me. Is your name (and then you make up any name)?" Then you say, "Oh, I thought you were so and so, but you're better-looking than he is." Then you go from there.

*Sally, 14*

I'll ask him if he's seen one of my friends. Like I may go up to a strange guy and say, "You know a girl named

Gi-Gi? She's the tall blonde who always wears a black leather jacket?" Then hopefully he'll start talking to me.

*Esther, 17*

I'll have my Walkman and I'll go up to him and ask him to listen to this tape for a minute. Then I'll ask if he likes that group or not.

*Tanya, 16*

I ask him for directions to somewhere. Like if we're in school, I'll ask if he knows where the nurse's office is.

*Betty, 17*

If a guy isn't smiling, I'll go right up to him with this real sweet, sympathetic look and say, "Why are you looking so sad?"

*Nadine, 14*

I'll go up and tell him my friend thinks he's cute and she wants to know his name. In the meantime I'm the one who thinks he's cute and I've found out his name. Later, after we talk, he usually starts liking me and says, "Forget your friend" (the one who never existed).

*Edith, 17*

These girls are great. They have plenty of ideas. I'll bet you have a few of your own. What's stopping you, now that you know that guys love it when girls start the conversation? However, just in case you're not ready to start a conversation with a guy, here's another idea. Why not try a simple compliment?

## HOW DO GUYS FEEL ABOUT COMPLIMENTS?

Guys thrive on compliments from the opposite sex. A guy will remember a sincere compliment from a girl for a long time. When I asked guys the compliments they've gotten from girls, they recalled every last one of them. Here's what they say:

Girls have said I'm fun to be with, I'm smart, and I'm good-looking. When a girl compliments me, it improves my self-image. It makes me feel relaxed and attracted to the girl.

*Joe, 16*

"You have a great body," "You're funny," "You've got style." When a girl is that honest with you and not afraid to express herself, you can believe her in more serious situations.

*Greg, 15*

One girl told me she liked the way I party and bug out, and she thought I have a good sense of humor. It was music to my ears. I felt that she was on my level.

*Gary, 16*

"I love the way you walk." It made me feel like a man, and I wanted to hang around her to hear some more of that good stuff.

*Bobby, 17*

Compliments about my looks are nice, but compliments about my personality are better because you can tell she really knows what you're all about. A girl told me I'm very sensitive and understanding.

*Steve, 17*

When this girl told me I was a great dancer, I got so souped up I started dancing wildly with her for the rest of the night.

*Dick, 17*

A girl once told me I'm very mature and understanding. I felt important—superior to other guys. I thought she was discriminating and could tell the difference between good and bad in a person.

*Sal, 18*

I've gotten compliments on my hair, eyes, teeth, body, etc. Yes. I love a compliment because I try to present a

21

handsome picture, and it's nice for women to acknowledge my efforts.

*Christopher, 19*

Everyone secretly hopes that he or she is special—different from anyone else. When you come along and give a guy a well thought out compliment, you are telling him that you recognize his uniqueness. Finally someone has recognized him for what he believes or at least wishes to believe to be true about himself. Furthermore, your own stock goes up in his eyes. After all, as Sal indicates, a girl must have insight in order to recognize the difference between him and other guys. In other words, he thinks you're intelligent for having noticed his finer qualities—especially if you're talking about his personality.

Compliments about ability or personality are more difficult to come up with, because they require deeper thinking on your part, but as Steve says, they're even more appreciated than compliments on physical appearance. This is especially true of guys who are obviously good-looking and probably constantly hear the same old "You're gorgeous" or "I love your eyes." Such a guy desperately needs to hear something about his heart, his mind, or even his soul. Even a compliment on his strong handshake, deep voice, or the twinkle in his eye would indicate that you're looking past the mere externals. I did this to a fellow just the other day, without planning it. I told him that he had intelligent eyes. He looked at me, puzzled and thrilled at the same time. "How can you tell?" he asked sheepishly. I thought about it a moment and said, "It's the alert expression in them." He smiled and looked as if he wanted to hug me. Needless to say, we got off to a good start.

See how much power you have to reinforce another person's self-esteem? It's hard to believe guys are so needy, but they are. Remember, however, the compliments must be honest, or they will fall to the ground as empty flattery. In order to give a sincere compliment, study the guy carefully. Think about what it is you really do like about him.

If you're going to talk about looks, try to do it in an original way that comes from paying close attention to what is special about his appearance. Don't just say "You look great." Pick something specific to comment on and then say something unusual about that physical quality. For example, if you like his eyes, you can say "Your eyes have such a deep, mysterious look to them that it makes me wonder what's going on behind them." If you're charmed by his sense of humor, instead of saying "You're funny," say something like "Your mind takes the strangest turns. I never know where you're going to end up, but I always know I'll laugh when you get there." If you're going to compliment something he does, instead of saying "You played a good game," say "I couldn't believe it, the way you shot right in there and got that basket. You moved like a bullet. No one could stop you." You'll be surprised how easy it is to make people feel good about themselves—and about you once you begin to talk about the possibilities. It's a lot of fun—especially when you see how well it works. Guys love the compliments so much. They keep coming back for more—even when you're no longer interested in them.

## WHY DO GIRLS ACT STUCK UP WHEN IN FACT THEY'RE INTERESTED?

If girls want to meet guys, and most of them do, why do so many of them not only refuse to talk to guys or compliment them, but behave in a way that makes a guy think they're not interested at all? I'll bet you know the answer. You've probably done it yourself at least once in your life.

Many potentially wonderful romances have been murdered at birth because girls have been taught to put on a façade with guys—to act indifferent even when they're dying to meet someone. So instead of being friendly to a guy they're attracted to, they give him the cold shoulder. Why do they do it? Here's what the girls say. Let's see if we can learn from their mistakes.

23

I didn't want him to think I liked him so I put on a big act—like I couldn't care less. I was trying to act conceited and stuck up so he would think I was hard to get—not easy.

*Maxine, 16*

I was embarrassed because all my friends were around so I thought I'd look cool and get nasty to him.

*Denine, 15*

I liked him but I was shy and I didn't know what to say so I just walked away.

*Trina, 15*

He was very good-looking and I thought he was conceited so I figured I ought to give him a hard time, since he probably thought he was God's gift to the world. Anyway, I figured he probably has a lot of girls and he's just using me as a stand-in. I didn't want to give him the satisfaction.

*Betty, 18*

I was suffering from PMS, and I was in a bad mood.

*Tracy, 18*

I had an argument with my mother and I was depressed so I acted mean, but later I was sooo sorry.

*Anne, 16*

I felt ugly that day. No makeup, bad hair, etc. I couldn't believe he meant it.

*Eilene, 16*

Let's analyze this. Some girls put on a big act because they're afraid if they're friendly, the guy will think she's available—and somehow the girls believe that even being approachable makes them look desperate. They are wrong. It is in fact good for a guy to think a girl is available. How else will he believe that he has a chance with her?

No one is saying a girl has to act desperate or jump all over a guy when he approaches and start confessing things like "I've always had a crush on you." Of course not. A friendly hello, a little smile, and an invitation to a conversation would do just fine. By pretending to be uninterested, a girl sends the message "You're wasting your time," and the young man is insulted. He moves on. If even the most good-looking guys are insecure (and they are), how much more the middle-of-the-roaders and the not-so-good-looking ones? Can you imagine what they go through?

Of course some girls reject guys who approach precisely because they're so good-looking. It isn't fair to assume a guy is conceited just because he's handsome. Instead of holding his looks against him, why not feel complimented by the fact that this guy obviously thinks you're worthy of his attention? Otherwise, why would he be trying to talk to you?

Then there are the girls who are unkind to guys they're attracted to because they have PMS or are in a bad mood. By being so negative, they ensure that they will remain in that state of mind. Wouldn't it be better to be pleasant? After all, wouldn't a new romance—or friendship—be one way of shaking off the blues?

One girl admits that she rejected a guy because she felt "ugly" that day. But had she stopped to think about it, she would have realized that his paying attention to her on a "bad day" was much more of a compliment than if he had tried to speak to her when she looked her best. He must be able to see beyond the surface and to appreciate her for inner qualities. What a find he is—or could have been. If this happens to you, I advise you to be congenial, and not to apologize for the way you look. Guys look for something entirely different in a girl's appearance from what girls realize. We'll end the chapter with that discussion. In the meantime . . .

## HOW DO GUYS FEEL WHEN A GIRL LIKES THEM BUT PRETENDS SHE'S NOT INTERESTED?

Even though girls don't intend to insult the guy who's trying to get to know them, much less drive him away, that's exactly what they do. Boys become angry when they feel as if a girl is sending a double message. They feel—and they're right about this—that a girl who has indicated she's interested and then responds to an approach with an icy stare has no idea how much courage it requires to make that first move. As you'll hear in their own words, they're usually not willing to give a girl a second chance.

I feel sad and awkward. It seems that she's making a fool of me. Later, even if I find out for sure that she likes me, I would probably not go out with her because she's most likely two-faced.

*James, 17*

Disappointed, honestly. It's a turn-off because if I show I like her, why must she play games? She's acting like a kid. All she has to do is talk to me if she likes me. If she doesn't, I would stop trying.

*Gene, 15*

I really hate that. It upsets me. I tell those girls "Play Lotto. Don't play me."

*Darryl, 16*

I would lose all interest in the egotistical ___!

*Pete, 18*

Some guys catch on and realize it's a game, but most guys just move on.

*Herbert, 17*

I feel rejected, and I put on a forget-her attitude, even if I still like her.

*Joshua, 17*

At best, guys feel sad, awkward, disappointed, and rejected. At worst, they feel turned off, angry, and even furious enough to call her names. As Herbert says, some guys would be able to see through the pretense and realize it was just a game, but most guys would move on—including guys

26

like James, who would lose interest even if he realized she did like him. Isn't it better to just be yourself?

## WHAT SHOULD A SHY GIRL DO?

Some girls are not putting on an act when they fail to respond to a guy's attempt to make friends. They really *are* shy. I asked guys to tell these girls how to respond if someone asks for their phone number or tries to start a conversation, and they're embarrassed or nervous about this kind of attention from the opposite sex. Listen to these guys give advice:

If he asks for her number, give it to him but also tell him she's shy. Then he can make her feel more comfortable.
*Ryan, 16*

If she's that shy, she should find out a way to give him the number on the sly, like slip it in his notebook or something.
*Danny, 17*

If a girl is shy, when I try to start a conversation, instead of looking away or looking down, she should look at me and just say hi. I'll take it from there.
*Caesar, 18*

Guys like shy girls. If I try to talk to her and she doesn't know what to say, she can always ask me questions about school or something—just to show that she's not unfriendly.
*Robert, 15*

Aren't they sweet? Every guy I asked (and there were hundreds) advised the same thing. By all means, one way or the other, if you're interested, give him your number or talk to him. He won't hold it against you if you're shy.

27

# SUCCESS STORIES: BOY MEETS GIRL

How do teenagers meet each other and start going out in real life? I asked some teens to tell me how they met their current flame. Here's what they said:

We met in my English class. I remember telling my friend he's so cute. Many times I would look at him and he would speak to me, but I never thought we would become more than friends—I just didn't think he would feel the same for me, so I left it alone. Suddenly, one day he came over and sat next to me. Before you know it we exchanged phone numbers. The rest is history.

*Jennifer, 16*

I met my boyfriend at a dental office where I work. One day he came in and had a cleaning, and I couldn't stop looking at him. My heart was beating faster than ever, and I knew that he was looking at me, too. On his way out he asked me for my name and I told him. The next time he came in he said he would like to take me out, so I gave him my number. Now we've been seeing each other for four months.

*Yvette, 15*

I met my boyfriend on a blind date. At first I didn't find him attractive, but we went to an amusement park and had such a good time that I thought maybe I was wrong about him. The next time I ran into him was by chance, at a party. Now things had changed. He looked so good, and sparks were flying between us. We danced almost every dance. After that, we started going out. We're really in love now.

*Jessica, 16*

When I met David, he was playing PACMAN and I challenged him. He actually beat me. After the game we began talking about different things. Then he told his friend he liked me and his friend told my friend. The next time we saw each other he asked for my number and we started seeing more and more of each other. We've been together over a year now.

*Karen, 17*

And here's one from a guy:

I was playing in a basketball game, but just before the game I looked into the stands and saw a beautiful girl. I said to myself, "How will I play? I can't keep my eyes off her." I couldn't make one shot because I was so obsessed with her. After the game I was the first one dressed and up the stairs by the exit. Then I saw her making her way through the crowd. I stuttered when I tried to speak, but she said: "You played a great game." Then I said, "Thank you," and we talked for a while. Finally she was my girl.

*Waverly, 16*

You can meet guys anywhere—in school, at a part-time job (imagine if you worked in a sporting goods store!), through a blind date, at a game, not just at parties and discos. But notice that each of the preceding stories contains a common element. The girl was helpful when the guy made his approach. She cooperated by smiling, giving her telephone number, and in the case of stuttering, nervous Waverly, giving him a compliment. See how easy it is, girls. It's the guys who are really on the spot. Not you. So have a heart and help them out.

## OTHER KEYS TO ATTRACTING THE OPPOSITE SEX

If you give the impression that you're generally enjoying life, a guy will be attracted to you. No one is attracted to a depressed-looking person. Also, learn to be a little daring. Whenever you see a guy you like, why not walk right up to him and give him a friendly "Hi"? Then tell him your name and ask his. Why should he be offended if you do that? Are you offended if someone speaks to you in a polite way? Of course not.

Another good idea is to ask for help in something you know he's good at. Why not ask a smart guy to help you with your math or a strong guy to help you carry something? Guys feel important when you ask for their help. It makes them feel manly. You could ask someone you're interested in getting to know better to teach you how to swim, run faster, work out in the gym, play handball, change a tire, play the guitar, and so on. When one person takes on the responsibility of teaching something to another, the "teacher" forms a caring bond for the "student." That's a good start—isn't it?

Finally, if you're anything like me, you can be devilish. Go up to a guy you like and ask him why he's always staring at you. Tell him he makes you nervous and to please cut it out. (In the meantime, the guy never looked at you in the first place.) Then, the next time you see him, start laughing and say, "See what I mean. You're always looking at me." (By laughing, you keep him off balance. He doesn't know for sure if you're kidding or not.) The next time you see him, he will look at you. When he does, say "See what I mean. You're staring at me again." Then he'll laugh, too, and you may get into a conversation. If not; nothing lost. At least *you* had fun; if he didn't, it probably means the two of you don't share a sense of humor and wouldn't have a good time together—so you're lucky you found out early.

## DO GUYS LIKE TEASED HAIR, SEDUCTIVE CLOTHING, AND LOTS OF MAKEUP?

Girls often wonder why guys approach them when they're "looking their worst." Well, worst to a girl may be "best" to a guy. Guys like a natural look, even if you think it's dowdy. Here's what guys said when asked "When you see a bunch of girls hanging out together, which one would you pick if you had to go by the way she dressed and wore her hair and makeup?''

I like the one with the silky hair who doesn't really wear a lot of makeup, especially a lot of eye makeup, and I like the girl who dresses preppie.

*Mike, 16*

I can't deal with tacky—like a baseball hat or basketball sneakers, or dirty or mismatched clothes that are wrinkled or smelly, or anything too kinky, like a nose ring or humongous earrings. You could be Miss America and these things would turn me off.

*Nick, 17*

Her clothes would have to be casual, not too flamboyant—baggy clothes are cool, so I can wonder what's inside—and not too much makeup. I like to see a girl's face, not a mask. I don't like a girl who has unnatural-looking hair. A one-minute hairstyle is best.

*Martin, 16*

I would pick the one who's modestly dressed with no makeup because it shows me she's confident in who she is and probably has a great personality. I definitely want to meet her.

*Hamilton, 18*

I would pick the one that's dressed conservatively and neat. Her makeup should be nice, not like Mrs. Munster.

*Charles, 17*

If she's got on a pretty shirt or blouse with slacks, not too tight, and is neat and sweet-smelling, with a natural look (not too much makeup plastered on her face), I'd want to meet her.

*Leo, 16*

Even if a girl is beautiful, if she dresses slutty, with tight clothes and a too-short miniskirt, it turns me off.

*Thomas, 15*

Apparently, to a guy, less is more. They see excessive makeup, overly teased hair and ultra-tight, short clothing as a barrier. Guys are looking for warmth and friendliness in a girl's appearance, and when they see a painted look instead, they are put off.

In conclusion, the way I see it, girls would have a lot less trouble meeting guys if they would just do what comes naturally—in all areas of life. If they feel like smiling, they should smile. If they want to talk to a guy, they should do so. If they think of complimenting a guy, they shouldn't hold back out of fear of giving him a "swollen head." And if a good-looking guy approaches them, instead of putting on an aloof act, they should be friendly and receptive. Naturalness of appearance is also a plus. Girls who hide behind a lot of makeup and tease their hair for hours would be more appealing to guys if they let their natural beauty shine through.

And finally, I think girls should realize that guys are even more afraid of rejection than they are—and with good reason. Because they are usually the ones to make the first moves, they get rejected a lot more often than girls do.

## REMINDERS

1. Smile. Guys love a friendly smile and appreciate it even if they're not attracted to you. If you do smile, they will take notice of you, and, who knows? Anything can happen next.
2. Guys appreciate it when a girl starts a conversation with them. Often they don't know what to say, and in addition, they fear rejection. When a girl is the one to break the ice, it puts them at ease and makes them believe they have a chance of going out with her.
3. Guys love honest compliments and store them up in their minds—forever. When complimenting a guy, study him carefully and say something different about his looks or personality. He'll think you're intelligent for having no-

ticed, and he'll love you for making him feel good about himself.

4. Some girls act stuck up because they think if they show a guy that they like him, he will lose interest, but the opposite is true. Guys like girls who are warm, open, and friendly, and they feel rejected, angry, and offended when girls put on an act and behave in a cold manner. Nine times out of ten, if a girl plays hard to get, the guy will move on and no romance will take place.

5. Most guys prefer a natural look to lots of makeup, teased, stiff hair, and overly seductive clothing. Take advantage of this fact and develop your own style of dress. Why cover up your natural beauty?

# 3

# How to Keep a Guy Coming Back for More

Now that you've got his attention, how do you keep it? What is it in a girl that makes a guy want to be around her more and more rather than less and less?

Let's start out with what *not* to do. No matter how beautiful, sexy, well groomed, and well dressed you are, there are some surefire ways to make sure your relationship with a guy doesn't last more than a week or two. All you have to do if you're really serious about getting rid of someone is talk about yourself and only yourself every moment you are together. You can start out by bragging about the great things you've done and all of the wonderful guys you've gone out with before him, and then you can start talking about your many problems. You can even get into details about all of the people who've "done you wrong" and how much you hate the world. If by any chance that doesn't work, you can take the opposite tack and sit there sullenly, refusing to say a word. Let him do all the talking, but don't react to anything. Just give him a "deadpan" face. If he says anything funny, don't laugh, and never, ever do anything spontaneous or offbeat. Be totally cool—like a dead fish. Never get deep about anything. Keep it all superficial. If he ever tries to talk to you about your personal beliefs—

religious, political, or whatever—laugh it off and act as if you think it's stupid to think about such things. Finally, never do anything together other than make out and listen to music or watch TV or videos. If he suggests doing something that he likes, go on the assumption that you couldn't possibly have any interests in common with him. And never ever invite him to do anything with you. Assume he is as uninterested in your life as you are in his.

That's what *not* to do, but that's not what this chapter is about. It's a chapter on what to do. In this chapter you'll find out what it is guys love in a girl and what they're starving for. What's more, you'll discover that you can easily give it to them and that you'll enjoy doing it (and it's not what you may be thinking). You'll learn how to make yourself important to a guy by taking an interest in his accomplishments and being concerned about his problems. You'll find out how to ensure that the guy is never bored with you, as you allow your natural enjoyment of life and sense of humor to emerge. You'll discover how doing things together can bring you closer together in spirit. You'll find ways to discover which values you share, a discovery that can either help you to form a stronger emotional bond or encourage you to break one that obviously isn't right for you.

In the process of doing all of these things, you'll discover that the guy you are interested in not only reciprocates by seeking out your company, but that he will also begin to take a greater interest in you—in your accomplishments, problems, concerns, and values. In other words, the goal of this chapter is to help you to have a more satisfying relationship with the guy in your life, whether he's there for the short term or the long term.

## WHAT GUYS LOOK FOR IN A DATE

I asked guys to tell me what traits they look for in girls they date. For some this means going steady, while others don't feel ready to give up playing the field—but for all of them the qualities that mattered most had to do with personality and character.

She should be as interested in me as I am in her. When I do something, I want to think that she can't wait to hear about it, not that she's bored to death with things in my life.

*Ricky, 17*

I want her to be thoughtful and caring—for example, if something is bothering me, I would love it if she could tell, and if she helped me to get it out in the open. I mean, I wouldn't want to bother her with it, but I would love to feel that it wasn't a bother at all.

*Brandon, 16*

She should be full of the devil. I mean, a funny girl who is always ready to play a trick or take a joke is the best company. Without a sense of humor, you're dead.

*Andy, 15*

For starters, she should be able to talk about more than just the latest hit album. If she can't get deep once in a while and let me know how she feels about things that are important to me, I'll wonder if she's an empty-headed ditz.

*Greg, 18*

I want to do lots of different things with the girl I go out with. If all she wants to do is sit around and mope, I'll quickly get bored with her. When we're together we should have fun and enjoy each other's company.

*David, 14*

You can see by their answers that guys are looking for a lot more than a physical attraction to a girl. They're seeking mental affinity and emotional compatibility. They want someone to laugh with and to cry with—someone to have fun with and someone to complain about life with. They want someone to share not only their adventures but their ideas as well. In short, they really don't want just a sex object. They want a friend and a partner—kind of a "comrade."

## TAKE AN INTEREST
## IN HIS ACCOMPLISHMENTS

One of the things I heard most frequently when I interviewed guys about what they wanted in a girlfriend was someone who appreciated what was special about them. They need to feel valued for their achievements and supported in their ambitions and goals—not pushed to be something they're not. Girls who are genuinely interested in them are the ones they look for. Why? Let's see what they have to say.

I take it as a compliment if a girl acts happy about something I've done. It shows me she cares about things that are important to me. It means she cares about me.

*Paul, 16*

When a girl appreciates my hard work, I know she's not only out for herself. Then I think about her accomplishments, too, and I start taking an interest in her in a real way.

*Jordan, 17*

When a girl is excited about something I've achieved, I feel proud of myself—I know that what I do pleases her and it shows me she's not self-centered.

*Doug, 17*

Being recognized in a special way encourages me to do even more. In fact, it makes me feel happy about everything in my life—especially her—and I feel as if I always want to be around her.

*Phil, 16*

If a girl shares my feeling of accomplishment, it makes me think our relationship will last because I know I'll have her support any time I need it—and I know she likes me for what I am.

*Todd, 17*

It's no fun to achieve something if there isn't anyone to share the celebration with you. When you get excited about something a guy accomplished, what you're doing is telling him he's right to be excited—he's not a fool, what he did really *is* important.

Because people love to talk about the wonderful things that have happened to them, why is it that we don't simply make everyone happy by listening for hours on end? The answer is simple. Since listeners are human, too, and we also want to be heard, most of us wait impatiently for others as they tell us their good news, looking for the right time to interrupt them and break in with a story of our own. This is a natural inclination, but it can be overcome. Here's how:

A friend of yours comes running over to you with the news: "I studied all night and I pulled a 92 on my math test." You say: "That's nice. I got a 97." What *should* you have said? "Congratulations. Your hard work really paid off." For the moment, forget about yourself. After all, you can't expect your friend to be happy for you if you don't at least acknowledge his achievement first. If later your friend asks what you got and you tell him you got a 97, chances are he'll make a big fuss over how great you are, too. He won't mind saying something like "Wow. You're amazing," because he has been duly acknowledged.

Another example of the ways we sometimes spoil each other's good news, again using the case of the math test, is what often happens when one person has had disappointing news. Suppose your friend announces that he got a 92 and you say, "Man, I only got a 65. I made a lot of stupid mistakes." Your friend will probably feel guilty for telling you his mark, and he may make an excuse to change the subject, or he may think you're jealous of his mark because you didn't even acknowledge it. He didn't tell you his mark to put you down. All he wanted was someone with whom to celebrate his victory—preferably you. Had you controlled your initial response and thought about his needs for a moment, you would have congratulated him and thereby given him the psychological gratification he needed. Then, if you wanted to, you could still have told him about your low mark without spoiling things for him. Who knows? He might have volunteered to tutor you in math. But he would definitely feel indebted to you for your willingness to forget about yourself for a moment and concentrate on him.

This principle can be applied to boyfriends on a regular basis. Guys accomplish things all the time. They make teams (football, baseball, soccer, and so on), win races or games (or at least help their teams to win them), get coveted jobs, are accepted into colleges, make speeches, do good works in their communities, save up and buy major items, pass difficult exams, put together singing groups, build things, and so forth. Think of a guy you're currently interested in or even a past boyfriend. What did he accomplish that you could have celebrated?

Be prepared for the future. What are some things your current boy-interest might accomplish in the near future? Think about what you can do to join in the celebration. Prepare to make a big deal of it. Get ready to control any initial reaction of boredom or jealousy, and to see things from his eyes. Here's what happened to sixteen-year-old Carol who did just that.

My boyfriend is in a rock band. They entered a competition in California, which meant he would be gone a whole week. I was a little jealous and worried that he would cheat on me. One night he called me and I could hear the noise of loud music in the background. He said they had won the competition. My first reaction was to skip right over that and ask him if he was cheating on me and partying, and if he really missed me—but I caught myself. Realizing how excited he must be about winning, I forced myself to say "Fantastic. I'm so happy for you. You guys deserve it. I know how hard you worked." Then

I asked some questions about the details of the competition. By the time he hung up his voice had gotten serious and he said: "I love you. I really miss talking to you. You're the only one who understands me." In the meantime, if I had done what I wanted to do and started quizzing him about other girls, we probably would have had a fight or he would have made an excuse to get off the phone.

It takes a lot of discipline to put aside our own needs for the moment and project ourselves into the mind of someone else in order to meet that person's needs, but it's not impossible. All you have to do is pretend you are that person and ask yourself, "If this were me, what would I need to hear? What kinds of comments would be music to my ears? What kinds of questions would I wish someone would ask me?" Then you'll know what to say. It's that simple.

In fact, think of a time when someone did react appropriately to one of your achievements. Wasn't it wonderful? Didn't you appreciate it and feel warmly toward that person? Aunts, uncles, and best friends are good at this. They seem to have a gift for getting excited about the accomplishments of those they love. In fact, they get so excited, you would think the wonderful event happened to them.

You can learn to do this for others, specifically, for your boyfriend or a guy you're interested in. If you become the main person to celebrate a guy's accomplishments, who will be the first person he calls when something good happens to him? You, that's who. Not those who he knows will say "That's nice" and begin immediately talking about themselves.

## LISTEN TO HIS PROBLEMS

Why do guys tend to fall in love with girls who listen to their problems? For the same reason people often fall in love with their therapists. Apparently, a very special bond is formed between the sympathizer and the teller. I asked guys to tell me how they feel about girls who are compassionate and who listen with understanding to their problems. They said:

When a girl cares about my troubles, I know our relationship has gone way beyond physical attraction.

*Sean, 16*

It makes me feel that I'll always have someone there when I'm depressed or sad. I'll love her because she supports me in my time of need.

*Kyle, 17*

I feel closer to her because I know I'm not alone, and that she'll be with me through good and bad times. I wish I could find a girl like that. She would be my best friend.

*Anthony, 18*

That would be the most beautiful thing she could do—listen and understand. It would make me feel I could talk to her about everything. I'd know who to talk to about problems in my life.

*Aaron, 17*

When you listen with concern and compassion to a guy's problems, he is forced to look past the externals—your looks. As Sean says, he begins to realize that his attraction for you is a lot more than physical. It's mental and emotional as well. The guy begins to think of you as someone he can trust. His loneliness and isolation are lessened, and suddenly the problem at hand is not so terrible, because there's someone with whom he can share it. Who wouldn't be tempted to fall in love with someone who could do that for him?

Listening to other people's problems is easy. You don't have to come up with solutions or provide expert advice; your sympathetic ear is enough. After all, the spotlight is not on you and your wisdom, but on the person and his problem. You do the comforting, but the other person does most of the talking. There's no pressure on you whatsoever.

In order to be a good listener, focus your eyes on the person who's speaking; if you let your eyes wander around the room, you'll be indicating that you're bored and don't really want to hear what's being said. Because most males strive to appear self-sufficient and tough, any hint of boredom or impatience will stop a guy cold. He will suddenly realize he's been exposing his emotions to someone who isn't even interested—hence making a fool of himself.

As your boyfriend speaks about his problem, at appropriate times, even if you have nothing else to contribute, nod your head and interject such phrases as "I see what you mean," "Mmm-hmmm," or "Oh, no." Then, as you listen carefully, try to articulate for him the feelings he is expressing, in your own words. If he's very angry about a disagreement he had with a teacher or a parent, you can say something like "You must have felt like slamming the door right in her face," or "I'll bet you had to use a lot of self-control when he said that," or, if he's been telling you about his parents' divorce, you could help bring his feelings out by saying something like "You must have felt very sad and alone when your father left." He may then answer, "That's *exactly* how I felt," or some such thing, indicating that you've touched his precise emotions—and that he's relieved that someone understands what he went through. At that moment, he will have moved closer to you emotionally, because you are that someone who made him feel not alone in the world.

The idea is to pick up on his inner feelings and give him a chance to air them by stating them for him out loud—but not in such a way that you appear to be judging him. For example, if he's angry, you wouldn't want to say "You're so angry, you'd better calm down before you have a heart attack." Instead you would say something like "I'll bet you're angry enough to punch through a wall." If he appears frustrated, you wouldn't say "Oh, don't waste your energy. It's a hopeless case." Instead you would say "It sounds to me as if you've had about all you could take of these people." Sadness and hurt are especially difficult for guys to express, which may make them particularly grateful to anyone who can help them get such feelings out into the open.

By helping someone put his feelings into words, calmly and objectively, without judging him, you provide him with much-needed relief. Although his problem is still there, he at least is comforted in that he no longer feels alone in it, and you'll probably be the first one he seeks out the next time he has a problem that no one else seems to understand. Why wouldn't he? Think about it for a moment? Wouldn't you?

By now you might be wondering what's in this for you, besides the chance to hear someone's problems the next time he's in need of a shoulder to cry on. After all, you're not being paid to be a psychologist, and what about your needs. Don't you deserve to be listened to and sympathized with once in a while? Well, there's good news. Most people learn by example, so in time you'll find that your boyfriend begins doing unto you as you have done unto him. He'll begin listening to *your* problems with interest and compassion.

## HAVE A SENSE OF HUMOR

Why do guys like girls with a sense of humor? Apparently they're more fun to be with—more exciting and even unpredictable. Humor also helps to take the tension out of a relationship. Girls who can laugh at themselves make guys feel at ease about their own screw-ups. Let's see what the guys say:

If there's no fooling around, the relationship gets dull. My girl is always playing some trick on me. For instance, we were at a party and I had been introduced to so many people I had forgotten their names. But there was one guy who had just told me his name and I had already forgotten, so I asked my girl on the sly what it was. His name was Jimmy, but she told me it was Bart. I then called him Bart and he looked at me like I was crazy and started laughing. "Bart, my name is Jimmy." My girl was doubled over in the corner laughing. She's too much.

*Jorge, 16*

One day I went over to my girl's house and she offered me some iced tea. When I drank it, suddenly I noticed my shirt getting all wet in the front and I was embarrassed. I thought I was dripping it as I drank, and I tried to hide it, but I kept dripping and the wet spot got larger and larger. Finally I asked her for a napkin. She yelled at me and said, "What's the matter with you? Didn't you learn how to drink without spilling?" Then she showed me that the glass had hidden holes in it. It was one of those trick glasses. We both started cracking up.

*Justin, 18*

You can relax when your girl is funny. I can always count on her to lighten things up. One day I asked her to clean my sneakers and she got annoyed because she said it wasn't her job. I went to the bathroom, and when I came back, she had filled my shoes up with soap suds. They were floating in the kitchen sink. I wanted to get mad, but it was so funny I couldn't help laughing. I ended up taking her sneakers and running up the block with them—with her two feet behind me, beating me on the head with my wet sneakers.

*Gary, 17*

My girlfriend has a lot of spice. I'll never forget the time she was acting silly and started a lemonade fight with me. We were soaking wet and sticky and on the floor splitting our sides laughing. After that I felt closer to her for some reason. I mean, I just liked her more.

*Billy, 18*

A girl who can give and take a joke is more lovable than a serious girl. My girlfriend invited me over to her house when her mother wasn't home. She made a big thing out of it, so I got the idea that we were finally going to have sex. When I got there, she had all the cleaning stuff out and she was in work clothing. She put a mop in my hand and I ended up cleaning her house with her. Although I was disappointed, I couldn't help but laugh and think "Man, is she crazy. That's what I get for thinking along those lines." She's too much.

Ellis, 16

Even though I'm a typically serious guy, I like a girl to laugh and have fun. I remember one day when I was walking with my girl and she slipped and fell right on her butt. She looked at me and broke out into this laugh. I was impressed because most girls would have gotten all embarrassed and upset.

Pepe, 17

When a girl can lighten things up, it puts a guy at ease—makes him feel as if he can be himself. He's not afraid to make a mistake or say something wrong because he knows she'll have a sense of humor about it instead or rejecting him.

There's excitement in humor because of its unpredictability. When a guy never knows what his girl is going to "pull" next, it keeps his adrenaline up. Going out with such a girl is an adventure. He wants to come back again and again to find out what's going to happen in the next chapter.

By now you may be thinking "But I don't have a sense of humor." Yes, you do. Everyone does. But many of us are afraid to express our sense of humor for fear of looking foolish. If you feel this way, the best advice I can give you is to say life is too short to worry about what other people think. Take the chance. Most people will appreciate a break from the seriousness of life. If you don't think this is true, ask yourself why comedians like Eddie Murphy, Arsenio Hall, Bill Cosby, and Rodney Dangerfield are among the highest paid of all entertainers and why they're in such demand.

## WHAT VALUES DO YOU SHARE?

If you want to get closer to your boyfriend, find out how he thinks. You can do this by asking a series of questions designed to bring out his values, beliefs, and goals—and to help him discover yours as well. Here's how to do that in "game" form.

Copy the following questions on separate pieces of paper and fold them up and put them in a bowl. Then each of you alternately pick out questions and ask them of each other. What you learn may be a big surprise.

1. If you were engaged to someone who became suddenly paralyzed for life, would you marry that person anyway? Why or why not?
2. Would you be willing to leave the United States forever if you were guaranteed an income of a million dollars a year for the rest of your life? Why or why not?
3. Do you believe in heaven and hell? What do you think happens to those who live an evil life?
4. What did you do in your life that you are most proud of?
5. What is the biggest mistake you ever made?
6. If you had the power to cure the world of AIDS forever, but you had to choose between that and becoming a multimillionaire, which would you choose and why?
7. Would you be willing to give up television for one year if it would somehow stop an earthquake in Iran that would take the lives of 5,000 people?
8. If someone killed your mother or father and managed to get away with it legally, what would you do?
9. If you had a choice of working at a job earning $45,000 a year in which you could also steal $100,000 a year with a guarantee of never getting caught, or working at a job where you could make $50,000 a year and not

have a chance of stealing anything, which would you take and why?

10. If you were forced to marry either one of these two, which would you marry and why: (a) An extremely good-looking, wealthy, sexy person who would treat you with continual indifference, or (b) a not-so-good-looking, middle-income, slightly overweight person who would adore you and treat you as if you were royalty? Why?

11. If you could know the date of your death, would you want to know? Why or why not?

12. If you had the power to kill people by writing their names on a piece of paper and burning it up, who would you kill, if anyone, and why?

13. If you had a chance between being instantly rich but not being allowed to do anything but travel, have fun, and party for the rest of your life, or continuing to live the life you are leading now, with the opportunity to pursue any goal you want but no guarantee of achieving it, which would you choose and why?

14. Which of your relatives do you admire most and why?

15. What is your happiest memory?

In addition to the questions I've supplied, you can also make up some of your own.

What are you going to find out by playing this game? You'll each find how the other feels about loyalty, family, country, honesty, religion, justice, good and evil, self-esteem, personal wealth, brotherhood, and love. In short, you discover what other each other "values" or believes in.

What's the purpose of finding that out? you might ask. Knowing more about each other can bring the two of you closer together or move you further apart, depending on your answers. If you find out that his values are in conflict with yours on basic issues, your feelings for him may change. If, on the other hand, you find out that you think alike, it may reinforce feelings of closeness and affection between you.

Say, for example, he responds to question 9 by saying he would take a job where he would be guaranteed the opportunity of stealing $100,000 a year without getting caught. After discussing his answer, you may find out that he believes there's nothing wrong with dishonesty, as long as you don't get caught. If this is how he feels, but you were brought up to value honesty, hard work, and integrity, you're likely to move away from him emotionally. In fact, you may begin seeing him in a different light because you will have lost respect for him.

But you're not planning to marry this guy, you say, so what's the big deal? Well, in order to be comfortable and happy with someone, in order for love to grow in depth, and in order even to be able to enjoy each other's company on any kind of a regular basis, there must be mutual respect. But if two people don't share at least some major values, they cannot respect each other.

If you do play the question game, be careful not to fall into the trap of arguing. When your boyfriend gives his answer, no matter how tempted you are to become angry with him if he totally disagrees with you, control yourself and listen to him instead. It's the only way you'll learn how he thinks. *Let him talk.* Then when you're alone, you can think about what he's said and come to your own conclusions. Even if you are diametrically opposed to his values, chances are you won't drop him right away. It will take a little longer for you to do that, but from that day on you will be mentally testing him in various situations, and each test he fails will be a mark against him until you finally feel as if you don't want to be around him any more.

But who says it has to end up that way? It may go the other way completely. You may find out he shares your values and the two of you think alike. If this happens, you'll feel closer to him, be more affectionate, and want to spend even more time with him. You'll have more in common than just superficial attraction. You'll have a spiritual bond as well.

## BECOME INVOLVED WITH HIS INTERESTS— AND SHARE YOURS

It's no mystery why guys like to go out with girls who enjoy doing the same things they enjoy doing. It's a good idea to try things he likes, such as going to a baseball game or even shooting baskets with him, even if at first you can't imagine yourself enjoying them. You may end up liking the activity long after you've lost interest in the boyfriend. If you like hiking, rock climbing, or horseback riding, encourage him to try it with you, and if the two of you have never gone skiing (or whatever), why not try it for the first time together? The new experience will give you a memory to share that can never be duplicated. After all, one can only do something for the first time once!

Another way to get closer is to work on a joint project, such as running an election in school or conducting a fundraising drive. You can also do simple things, such as going clothing or holiday shopping. If you go to a movie, instead of just saying "Wasn't that great?" after the show, talk about how you felt about specific scenes in the movie. Every shared experience is a golden opportunity for you to get closer to your boyfriend.

## BE YOUR BEAUTIFUL, NOT YOUR UGLY, SELF

We all have the potential to be either mean-spirited or magnanimous. We can gossip, express jealousy toward others, and be cruel and uncaring, or we can refuse to say a negative thing about another person, celebrate other people's successes, and be kind and compassionate. Most guys appreciate a girl who is generous rather than judgmental. If you want a guy to fall in love with you, don't gossip and backbite. He'll lose respect for you—and he'll wonder what you say behind *his* back. If you want him to think highly of you, don't express jealousy for other girls who you think are prettier or sexier than you. Instead of putting them down by making catty remarks, express your true feelings openly.

Say "She's beautiful. I wish I had her long hair." But stop there. Don't put yourself down either by saying something like "Mine is so short and it looks like Brillo." No need to put yourself down just because someone else possesses a quality you admire. By openly recognizing the assets of other girls, you'll gain the respect of your boyfriend. Girls who are friendly to other girls who are potential competition demonstrate self-confidence.

In any case, do you actually believe for one moment that by saying something negative about a pretty girl, such as "but look at her thunder thighs," your boyfriend is suddenly going to notice something he hadn't seen before, or cease being attracted to her? Of course not. All he's going to do is say to himself (about you): "She's jealous."

If you have an impulse to be kind or generous to others, don't suppress it. There's no need to put on a cold, hard exterior in front of your boyfriend. In fact, when a guy sees his girl being cruel or insensitive, he usually wonders, "will she treat me that way someday?" If you go to a movie and the character is suffering, and you feel like crying, don't hide your feelings and joke about the person's pain. Cry. You'll feel better and he'll feel better about you. If you see a homeless person and you feel the urge to give him some change, don't worry that your boyfriend may think you're a "sucker." Give in to your compassionate impulse. And if your boyfriend should make a callous comment about the homeless (or any other issue, for that matter), don't feel obligated to agree with him to save face. Instead say what you're thinking and let it go at that. Your feelings are yours and there's no denying them—or arguing about them.

A guy won't always tell you how much of an impression being warm, loving, generous, and generally magnanimous has on him, but it does. Men love kind women. In a way it's easy to understand. After all, it's the mother who has the complete power over her child (in this case her son) as he's growing up. As you know, the same power is not afforded to a father over his daughter or son.

Another reason many guys appreciate and feel comfortable with kind, caring women is their own difficulty in expressing their more gentle side. When a loving woman takes the lead, it becomes easier for a guy to reveal that he is sensitive.

In conclusion, be yourself and you'll do just fine. When you think about it, it's when we try to cover up, to put on airs, to pretend to be what we're not, that we get in trouble, because in the end, we can't back it up. People can see sincerity a mile away. It's a rare and treasured quality, one that in itself has the power to make you very attractive to the opposite sex—not that that's the only reason for being true to yourself. I can't imagine living any other way. Can you?

## REMINDERS

1. Guys are inclined to be attracted to girls who are interested in their accomplishments and who are willing to listen to their problems with an understanding ear.
2. Girls with a sense of humor keep guys coming back for more because they are unpredictable and exciting.
3. In order to form a stronger bond with a guy, talk about your mutual values. But be warned, this discovery can also drive you farther apart. If this happens, it's probably for the best.
4. Participate in a variety of activities together—things he likes, things you like, and things neither of you have ever done before. Keep the relationship fun and exciting.
5. Don't be afraid to let your tender, sensitive, compassionate side shine through. Men in general fear "cold-hearted" women, and even if they laugh off your cruelty to others, they secretly worry, "Someday will she do that to me?"

# 4

# Falling in Love . . . And Falling Out!

You've heard the expression, Love is what makes the world go round. Well, even if it's not literally true, we do know that it's a lot easier to get up in the morning when we're "in it" and a lot more difficult to go to school or work when we're falling out of it. Romantic love: You can't live with it because it sets your head spinning and disturbs your tranquility—but you wouldn't want to live permanently without it because life would be sooo boring.

What is love? Why do people "fall in love"? And how do you know you're really in love? What's the difference between love and infatuation? Do guys feel the same way girls do when they fall in love? Why do people fall out of love? How can you end a romance without ruining a guy for other women for the rest of his life? These and other questions will be discussed in this chapter.

## WHAT IS LOVE?

There are all kinds of love: the unconditional love given by a mother to her child; the altruistic love expressed by those who care for the homeless, the sick, and the abused; and finally, the love we're talking about: romantic love.

What is romantic love? It's a combination of extreme physical attraction and intense spiritual attraction—an attraction that goes beyond the realm of friendship. When I speak of spiritual attraction, I'm talking about being drawn to that part of a person that makes him unique—the sum of his beliefs, principles, and values. In essence, I'm talking about his inner being or soul.

When two people experience such an attraction, the combination of spiritual and physical, they "fall in love." They feel drawn to each other as if by a powerful, irresistible magnet. They want to be with each other every moment of the day, to know everything there is to know about each other, to reveal their secret thoughts and desires to each other. The love-struck couple feel that they understand one another and are understood in a way that no one else has ever done for them, and they seem to accept each other for exactly what they are—for their uniqueness. They are convinced that nothing matters more than the love they feel, and they wouldn't give it up for the world. They feel as if they were literally born again.

## YOU CAN'T BE IN IT ALONE

Notice I speak in terms of "they," for the kind of love I'm describing *always* involves two people. One-sided love is just a "crush," and although it's painful, it's not the same as being "in love." In order to be "in love," you have to be "in it" with someone. You can't really be "in it" alone. If you love someone who does not respond to you, you feel frustrated rather than fulfilled. You don't feel special, because the one you love is not physically and spiritually attracted to you. You feel shut out and let down rather than elated and accepted. You feel angry—and even like a fool. That's not love. That's a one-sided crush.

When you're in love, you experience all sorts of strange changes. Your stomach closes up, you may not feel like sleeping at all, you're distracted, dreamy, flighty, and silly. All that really matters is being with the one you love. But it's not just physical—it's emotional and spiritual. And the physical attraction itself is much more than sexual, but at the same time it's very very physical. You want to hold each other and kiss and just talk for hours, regardless of whether you actually have sex. You are "in love," and it's wonderful.

## HOW DO GIRLS FEEL WHEN THEY'RE FALLING IN LOVE?

The following young ladies describe the feeling. See if it sounds familiar. Later we'll compare it to the way guys feel.

I can't eat, sleep, or concentrate, and when the phone rings, I jump. I make up excuses to see him and when I do, I blush.

*Fran, 15*

Like the whole world is beautiful and great—lots of energy, a high without drugs.

*Marthe, 16*

I feel happy and confident in myself—queasy and lightheaded. My heart beats 100 miles a second. Nothing could get me down.

*Joanne, 16*

He's on your mind night and day. You feel like butterflies are flying around in your stomach.

*Betsy, 18*

You get a knot in your chest and a warm feeling all over.
*Linda, 17*

I felt like I died and went to heaven in a garden filled with white roses.

*Tama, 15*

I feel like my whole life is changing. I swing back and forth from a joyful feeling to a fear that he may not love me anymore.

*Marva, 18*

I feel like I'm walking on air—on cloud nine, on top of the world. I'm nice to everybody around me. I feel like buying him gifts.

*Charlene, 16*

I'm mesmerized. When I'm not with him, I'm not depressed, but I'm waiting for the moment when we can be together again. When we're together, I'm planning every moment with him, and when I'm not, I'm talking about him to my friends.

*Susan, 14*

If so many people can describe the feeling precisely, there must be such a thing as "falling in love," and falling is just what it is, because just like the feeling of falling, love gives you the sensation of being out of control. Like falling, it's scary, because you can't stop what's happening. But even if you could stop it, would you? Why should you? You've probably never felt happier in your life.

## HOW DO GUYS FEEL WHEN THEY'RE FALLING IN LOVE?

Do guys feel the same way? Yes, and then some. I asked guys how they feel when they fall in love. They say:

Warm inside. I had another thing to get up for in the morning and someone to think about just before I went to sleep.

*Jeff, 17*

Great. Like I was on top of the world. Nothing could go wrong.

*Bruce, 15*

You're always happy and you'll do anything you can to make her happy. You feel really good inside.

*Scott, 16*

You always look forward to spending your next day with her—and you want to share everything with her.

*Joseph, 18*

Bewildered and confused. You don't know what's going on.

*Daimon, 17*

Like you never want to leave her, like she was sent by an angel.

*Martin, 18*

Full and drained at the same time. I couldn't stand to be apart from her. Like the world was mine. I couldn't tell one day from the next.

*Louis, 16*

Who says guys are not romantic? It seems to me they feel all of the same ecstatic, warm, out-of-control sensations that girls do, only they aren't as quick to talk about what they feel to their friends or even their girlfriends. This is easily understood when you think of the "macho image" our society expects from men (a subject I discuss at length in *The Opposite Sex is Driving Me Crazy*). But isn't it great to know that guys do have such tender feelings?

Don't worry, ladies. You're not "in it alone." Just like you, your boyfriends are likely to experience certain physical reactions to the excitement of being in love—a warm feeling inside, butterflies, a knot in the stomach, loss of appetite, dizziness, inability to sleep, and so on. But the similarity of the emotional reaction is even more compelling. When they're apart, both lovers wait only for the moment when they can be together again. They think of nothing but the loved one—day and night. Ordinary responsibilities seem unimportant and concentration is gone. They're so happy they don't know what to do with themselves. They live in a state of ecstasy, alternating occasionally with despair when feelings of doubt and insecurity invade, as they always do eventually, if only for a brief time. But which is real—the ecstasy or the despair? Can love ever last?

## IS IT REALLY LOVE OR JUST INFATUATION?

All the feelings described are very real. Whatever you feel, for that matter, is very real. Don't ever let anyone convince you otherwise. But the feelings just described are the beginnings of love—the part that is often referred to as "infatuation," or "puppy love." Sometimes those feelings deepen and grow into a more lasting love, and other times they fade away and disappear until you wonder what you were so excited about in the first place—and even feel embarrassed when you think of how you behaved, now that you're back in your right mind.

But even when love lasts, its ups and downs become less dramatic over time, allowing you to go about your daily business in a normal fashion. That is to say, eventually you will be able to eat, sleep, and concentrate on work. Don't worry—this doesn't mean you've fallen out of love; it just indicates that your love has grown to a deeper level. People who have been married for twenty years, and who are still in love, experience a security and depth in their love. The sparks still fly, but the love is now based on shared experiences, mutual respect, deep caring, and a sense of continuity and permanence.

When love doesn't last, why doesn't it? Usually it's because one person falls *out* of love. First we'll see how girls feel when they fall out of love, then we'll see how the guys feel. Then we'll put it all together and try to understand why people fall out of love.

## HOW DO GIRLS FEEL WHEN THEY'RE FALLING OUT OF LOVE?

Girls remember exactly how they felt when they were falling out of love. They say:

I start picking on anything he does—argue all the time. I don't want to be around him and find excuses to avoid him.

*Anne, 17*

Everything he does makes me sick. I feel guilty because I cheated him out of the time he could have been with someone else.

*Dawn, 16*

I'm glad when he doesn't call and I start looking at other guys and feeling trapped.

*Brenda, 14*

I act mean to him. He nauseates me—disgusts me. I don't want him to touch me. I wonder what I ever saw in him. Yuk. Get away.

*Liz, 15*

I'm depressed that I have to deal with him at all—annoyed at his presence, eager to rid myself of him.

*Marthe, 16*

## HOW DO GUYS FEEL WHEN *THEY* FALL OUT OF LOVE?

Do guys share the same "turned-off" feelings? They say:

When she's around, you pretend she's not. You want to hide from her. You don't want to be with her at all.

*Greg, 16*

She bores me to death and I cheat on her constantly.

*Anthony, 17*

You don't feel comfortable with her anymore.

*Benny, 18*

I stay away from her and I don't miss her—it's not like it used to be at first. I start to treat her differently, too—even mistreat her in a way.

*Tom, 15*

If you see her with another guy, you don't get mad.

*Freddie, 19*

You become very quiet when you're around her—don't talk as much as you once did. You just want to ride off into the sunset—far away from her.

*Carey, 17*

Girls pick arguments and become critical of their boyfriends. They start to feel repulsed by their boyfriends' physical presence. Boys, however, don't seem to have as strong a physical reaction. They simply want to get away from the girl, to end the relationship, and they will do anything they have to to accomplish that goal: make excuses for not seeing her, clam up when they're together or on the phone, encourage her to see other guys, and see other girls themselves. Guys are not as dramatic or emotional about falling out of love. With them, it's a practical matter. "Let me just get away," they think. Guys do become dramatic and emotional, however, when they're still in love and the girl stops loving them, but we'll talk about that later in the chapter.

## WHY DO BOYS FALL OUT OF LOVE WITH THEIR GIRLFRIENDS?

We know that people fall out of love, but wouldn't you like to know *why* your ex-boyfriend fell out of love with you? As you read the following statements, maybe you'll think of your own romantic life and understand a thing or two. I asked guys: "Why did you fall out of love with your ex-girlfriend?" They said:

She kept calling me every day—and wanted me to be with her twenty-four hours a day, seven days a week. I couldn't do anything alone. There she was. I got sick of it.

*Martin, 19*

She followed me everywhere. I mean, you like to be close to your girl, but not *that* close.

*Henry, 17*

I couldn't stand the way she sang in an opera soprano voice to the tunes of popular songs when we were in the car.

*Theo, 17*

She was in a bad mood all the time. I couldn't put up with it, and she was boring. All she wanted to do was stay home all the time.

*Jeff, 16*

She was always acting childish—always wanting to play and never be serious.

*Jose, 17*

She was very nosy and she did mean things too. I got sick of it.

*Ralph, 15*

She promised not to tell me major lies, but she did anyway. Also, she could never come out except to help me spend my money.

*Tony, 18*

She told me that when her ex-boyfriend broke up with her she tried to kill herself. I figured she must be a little out of tune.

*David, 18*

She criticized things I enjoy, like writing and using my computer, and acted like I was a nerd. I knew she wasn't right for me if she couldn't accept me for what I am.

*Mike, 16*

I wrote her a poem, trying to be romantic, and she made fun of me and read it in public to all of our friends.

*Smitty, 18*

She got overly confident and started bragging to her friends about our relationship.

*John, 15*

I got tired of her because she did everything I told her. I wanted a girlfriend, not a slave.

*Wally, 15*

After I had sex with my girlfriend, she wanted to get into a serious relationship and I wasn't ready for one, so I broke up with her.

*Elliot, 16*

Some guys trace their decision to break up with their girlfriends to qualities or traits that they find so annoying that they become blind to those qualities which attracted them in the first place. Theo got turned off when he heard his girlfriend's high-pitched singing voice. Jeff and Jose felt let down as they gradually discovered that their girlfriends' temperaments clashed with their own. It is important to realize that none of the girls did anything wrong. They were simply being themselves, but those "selves" had for some reason—almost certainly not the reasons cited by their boyfriends—ceased to be acceptable to those boys. This is something that happens frequently in romantic love: Without really understanding why, we fall out of love, and then all the energy and passion that we had formerly put into a adoring the loved one gets reversed, so that we become as irrationally repelled as we had earlier been attracted. No one is to blame for such a turn of events—neither the fickle lovers, nor the ones with the irritating singing voice or the playful ways. Love, especially in the early stages and at a young age, is very fragile. It can die without our ever understanding why, though we may, like Theo, Jeff, and Jose, try to find an explanaiton, however weak it may be. This is not to criticize those guys. They are sincere in their belief that they have put their finger on the problem. But love is psychologically more complex than they understand, and were their girls to stop singing, go out more, and be serious, love would still not be restored. So don't try to change the things that make you who you are in hopes of attracting—or keeping—a boyfriend.

That does not, of course, mean that you shouldn't listen to legitimate criticisms or ignore some of the common pitfalls of love. Some kinds of behavior *should* be changed. Possessiveness, for example, can kill many relationships. As Martin and Henry illustrate, some guys leave because they feel smothered. Even a fire needs air in order to continue burning. When their girlfriends demand that they spend every waking moment with them, the initial fire of love is extinguished.

Ralph, Tony, and John fell out of love because they found out their girlfriends didn't share their values. Ralph tired of his girlfriend's nosy, gossipy ways, Tony couldn't accept a girl who lied, and John's need for privacy and discretion was violated when his girlfriend talked too much to other people about their relationship. In cases like these, the girls might have done well to consider changing their behavior in order to try to hold on to their boyfriends.

One of the main reasons people fall out of love is the discovery that their love object does not, after all, value or enjoy them for what they are. Mike was disillusioned when his girl made fun of his writing and his love for computers, and Smitty was horrified when his girl was insensitive enough to air his romantic poem in public. She obviously had no respect for him or his feelings. Even if you do value your boyfriend for himself, however, he may feel pressured if he thinks you expect too much of the relationship. Elliott wasn't ready for a commitment (although his girlfriend probably felt that he was serious about her because he had sex with her). Wally, too, felt pressured, because his girlfriend was so slavish in her adoration of him. And David ran the other way when he realized he was involved with a girl who might threaten suicide if the relationship didn't work out. Imagine how frightened he felt when he heard that!

But even if you haven't put any uncomfortable pressure

on your boyfriend, it may just have been too early for him to commit himself to you. Maybe he felt as if he had to meet other girls because his growing up demanded it. As ridiculous as this may sound, I have to say it because it's true: Don't take it personally. You may be in every way the girl of his dreams and still lose him if he's not ready to settle down—as very few boys in their teens are.

## HELP! HE'S FALLING OUT OF LOVE WITH ME

How can you tell if your boyfriend is falling out of love with you—and how does it feel? Girls talk about this, as painful as it may be, in the hope that other girls will pick up the signs early so that they won't be shocked when the relationship ends. They also want other girls to realize that they're not alone. Most of us have experienced the loss of a boyfriend, and we live to tell it. I asked girls "How can you tell if a guy is falling out of love with you and how does this make you feel?" They say:

He doesn't spend as much time with you and doesn't like to talk on the phone—and he's not as affectionate. You feel sad and hurt.

*Marthe, 16*

He tries to brush you off and you do everything you can to make him love you again—but you know it's over. You feel let down.

*Deidre, 16*

He acts uninterested in what I'm doing or who I'm with. I feel like a fool—like the whole relationship was a waste of time and probably that it's my fault that he doesn't like me anymore. What did I do to push him away?

*Andrea, 17*

He avoids you. You feel lonely, abandoned, and upset.

*Mary, 16*

He begins to make comments about other girls and doesn't compliment me any more or take me places. I feel depressed, jealous, and hurt. I'm thankful to my friends who are supportive.

*Evelyn, 16*

He makes me wait for his call, but he never calls. I blame it all on me. I wonder what I did and how I could have changed.

*Sally, 16*

He acts different, like he has something on his mind. I feel like the victim of something I caused myself.

*Keisha, 16*

He tells me I'm getting on his nerves or he wants to be free to see other girls. I feel very angry, mad, confused, frustrated, and hateful.

*Nicole, 18*

He makes excuses when you ask him to go somewhere with you. You feel crazy—like you need him and don't want to let him go. You feel powerless.

*Linda, 17*

He starts yelling at me and picking on me for little things, and he doesn't kiss me goodnight anymore. I feel sad and alone.

*Ro, 14*

Notice the common theme here. The guys make themselves scarce. They don't want to spend as much time with their girlfriends—they make excuses and avoid them, and if they are with their girlfriends, they criticize them or talk about other girls. They don't want to call, but if they do, they don't have much to say. The simple fact is, their hearts are not in it anymore. They've fallen out of love.

This is definitely no fun. In fact, it's very, very painful. Like the girls just quoted, most of us go through a few stages when our love object falls out of love with us first.

We feel abandoned, lost, alone. Where is he? What happened? What did we do to lose him? Then we feel sad and disappointed. We had built up hopes for an endless, glorious relationship. We may even have fantasized ourselves married to him. We had gotten used to that warm, wonderful companionship—something to look forward to every day. When we start trying to figure out what happened, for lack of a better reason we blame ourselves, searching for things we might have done to turn him away. That makes us insecure about our own worth, maybe even angry at ourselves for all our mistakes and failures (regardless of whether there's anything at all for which we should blame ourselves). Finally, when we realize that we're powerless to change the situation, we become angry. We may feel we've been made to play the fool, and we may consider getting even with him if we dwell on it long enough.

All of these feelings are normal. After all, no one in her right mind can help feeling sadness, loneliness, and anger about losing something that gave her great pleasure and comfort. But it helps us to cope if we can separate ourselves from the immediate situation and think for a moment. People lose interest in each other for many reasons, and to blame ourselves for falling out of love or for no longer *being* loved is ridiculous. It could be personality traits, conflict of values, rejection of each other's interests, and so on. After all, how could you be happy with a guy who is constantly telling you to "pipe down," when you're used to being the life of the party? Wouldn't you rather find a new boyfriend who likes you for what you are instead of trying to win someone back who doesn't? How can you live happily ever after if your boyfriend lives and breathes for his rock band but you can't stand the sound of loud music, and he thinks that your interest in Irish folk music is really weird?

Just as there is no reason to be angry with yourself for not being different from what you are, there's no reason to be angry with your boyfriend for falling out of love with you either. Didn't you fall out of love a few times in your life?

Did it mean that the guy you fell out of love with was a bad person? Or that you were a bad person? Of course not.

But what can you do about the anger that you feel—for you probably *will* feel anger even if you know it's not rational? If your boyfriend has fallen out of love with you and wants to break up, should you seek revenge? Should you curse him out and tell him all about his faults? Should you look for ways to hit below the belt? No. As difficult as it may be, if you use self-control and try to be mature about it, you'll feel better in the long run—and he'll think better of you. Another way to look at it is, try to handle the situation with grace and style—in other words, with class.

What is class anyway? It's graciousness in handling life's difficult situations. You never regret it later if you behave with class, and you almost always come to regret it when you don't. We'll talk more about how to get over the loss of a boyfriend in Chapter 10. But for now, while you're still suffering you need to acknowledge that you can't dance without a partner in the dance of love. It definitely takes two. Once you realize you're out there on the floor without a partner, you'll walk away as gracefully as possible—maybe a little sad, but definitely a lot wiser. Perhaps you'll have learned something about relationships, and what's more about yourself, which will help you for the next time. And there will definitely *be* a next time. You may have heard the saying "You only fall in love once." Nothing can be further from the truth.

There's someone up the road for you who is right for you, someone who will make you wonder how you could have ever felt so intensely about the guy you're losing. Take it from me, Joyce Vedral, the endless romantic. I'm divorced. I won't tell you how old I am, but I will tell you that I still fall in love, still act like a fool, still suffer the pangs of a broken heart, and still go out there for another round with an adventurous spirit, knowing that one day I'll meet that special person. And if I don't, I can say I loved every minute of the adventure. We'll talk more about how to cope with the loss of an intense love in Chapter 10.

# WHAT DO YOU DO WHEN YOU FALL OUT OF LOVE WITH YOUR BOYFRIEND AND WANT TO DROP *HIM?*

For now, let's think of the reverse. How does the poor *guy* feel when his girlfriend falls out of love with him? I think I just read your mind. "Who cares about how the guy feels? Too bad for him." But think of it this way. Guys have feelings, too. They're just as vulnerable as girls, and in some ways even more so, because when a girl breaks up with a guy, he worries that he may not have been "man enough" to keep her.

Adult men remember *forever* a rejection or a romantic heartbreak that took place in the teen years, and it actually shapes their attitudes toward women for the rest of their lives. Think of it. All of those "tough" teenage guys—you know, the macho fellows who don't show any emotions (as well as the ones who are not so tough and who do show emotions)—are literally at your mercy. What should you do to make it easier for them?

If you fall out of love with a guy and want to end the relationship, be merciful. Have a heart. Think of the kindest, most caring way you can to let the guy down gently. Don't tell him what you see as the cold, hard truth about himself, listing all of his faults. Instead tell him that he's a wonderful guy and you'll always have a special place for him in your heart but . . .

You need some time apart . . . or

You think things are getting too intense. You're not ready for a deep commitment yet . . . or

We can still date but we should see other people, if it's meant to be, we'll end up together . . . or

We're very different people. We have different values and interests. We'd both be much better off with someone who shares our goals, and so forth . . . or

I'll always be there for you as a friend. It would hurt me deeply to lose your friendship, but I'm not feeling very romantic anymore . . . and so on.

The point is, be kind. Whatever you do, don't break up with him in front of his friends. Don't leave a message on his answering machine or with his parents. Don't just string him along and avoid him.

Don't send him a "Dear John" letter either. A "Dear John" is a "kiss-off" or good-bye letter. The expression was first used to describe farewell letters girls would send their boyfriends who were away for months at a time during World War II. If the girl got tired of waiting, or if she met someone else, she would send a "Dear John" letter that ended the relationship. Now, a girl with a long-distance boyfriend had a good excuse to write such a letter at that time. After all, what else could she do? Keep writing love letters until the guy came home, so he could find out that his girl had married another guy? She couldn't exactly place a telephone call to the trenches to let him know the truth. But unless there is no other way, it's always better to talk to a guy face to face. It may be difficult, but he'll appreciate the respect, and you'll feel a lot better about yourself if you do. Perhaps, after all is said and done, the best way to decide on how to end the relationship is to put yourself in his position. Think of how you would like someone to break up with you. What would be the kindnest, most considerate, respectful way to do it? Then follow your own advice. If you do that, you can't go wrong. And remember, by letting him down gently, you'll make it easier for him to fall in love again—and make him more likely to be kind to the next girl if he's the one to fall out of love. Isn't that what you hope some other girl is doing right now for the next guy you're going to fall in love with?

## REMINDERS

1. Romantic love is the powerful combination of physical and spiritual attraction. Both girls and guys feel "out of their senses" when they fall in love.
2. Romantic love is not "infatuation" or "puppy love."

It's very real. The question is, will it grow and deepen or will it fade?

3. People "fall out of love" for many reasons: They discover that they don't share each other's interests, values, and goals; they find that their personalities are incompatible; they find that they do not accept each other for what they are, and so on.

4. Falling out of love is the most normal thing in the world, especially in the teen years when you are first discovering what you really like, value, and respect in another person.

5. If your boyfriend falls out of love with you, you may at first feel abandoned, sad, and confused, and you may wonder what's wrong with you that you weren't able to hold on to him. Once you analyze the situation, however, you'll stop blaming yourself and realize that your lost love has nothing to do with your being a lovable person. You may also feel angry and be tempted to seek revenge. These feelings are normal, but when you come to think of it, you'll probably decide to handle the situation with dignity.

6. If you fall out of love with your boyfriend and want to break up, let him down gently. What you do and say to a guy now may affect his relationships with women for the rest of his life.

# 5

# How Sex Changes
a Relationship

To do or not to do—that is the question. But even if you've already "done," you'll want to read this chapter, because you'll find some answers to other questions that have probably puzzled you and your friends.

Why do relationships change so dramatically once sex enters the picture? Is the change for the better or for the worse? How do girls feel the day after they have sex with their boyfriends, how do guys feel, and is there a major difference in their feelings? If so, why? Why do guys so often break up with their girlfriends soon after having sex? Why do girls generally become more emotionally involved than guys once sex enters the picture? What advice do girls who've had sex give other teenage girls regarding this matter? If guys are honest, what advice would they give girls regarding sexual conduct? Is it possible or even advisable for a teenager to remain a virgin in the nineties? If you've already had sex, does that mean you must continue to do so?

These and many other questions regarding sex and relationships will be discussed in this chapter.

# HOW DO GIRLS FEEL THE DAY AFTER THE FIRST TIME THEY HAVE SEX WITH THEIR BOYFRIENDS?

For a girl, even in the nineties, the decision to have sex remains a big one. Once a girl makes that decision, she enters a new world—often, a very scary one. I asked girls to tell me honestly exactly how they felt the day after they first had sex with their boyfriends.

I felt as if I was rushed into it—but I was in love. Yet I felt guilty.

*Cammy, 17*

I felt cheap because I thought about what I did and I realized I wasn't ready for it.

*Carla, 16*

I felt strange and, in a sense, used. It was like we were both caring for the same person—him. I felt left out of it.

*Elizabeth, 15*

I felt angry. I had promised myself I would wait until I was married, but I did it anyway. Now it was too late. I had lost my virginity.

*Alice, 15*

I knew I had made the biggest mistake of my life. I felt stupid. I said I would never do it again, and I didn't.

*Chandra, 14*

I felt as if I had done something wrong. But aside from that, I felt stupid—ridiculous. I certainly didn't get any thrill out of it. It was embarrassing to say the least.

*Eilene, 16*

I worried, is he going to leave me? Did he go with me just to get what he wanted?

*Anne, 19*

I had mixed feelings. In a way, I thought I did it out of love, but then I was afraid I would get pregnant.

*Kay, 16*

I felt like God wasn't going to forgive me. I asked myself again and again, "Why on earth did you do it?"

*Nancy, 17*

I was happy, but all I could think of was, "Will we be together forever, or was he just unloading himself on me?"

*Fanny, 16*

I felt I would love him for the rest of my life because we had waited a long time (eight months) and losing my virginity to him was special.

*Sharon, 17*

Sex can and should be a wonderful experience. If that is so, why did only a few girls express undivided joy over it? Why did so many feel used and even abused? The majority of girls interviewed expressed feelings of guilt, fear, anger, resentment, insecurity, and disappointment. And why didn't even one of them mention getting a physical thrill?

Obviously, the girls just quoted were not "ready" for sex. But why not? One problem was physical—their bodies were not mature enough to enjoy the pleasures of simply sex. As I discuss at length in my book, *The Opposite Sex Is Driving Me Crazy,* during the teen years, guys have a much higher sex drive than do girls and are much more easily aroused. Their hormones are literally going wild, and a sexual encounter for them is usually satisfying physically, regardless of their own level of experience—or their partners. Women, on the other hand, generally do not reach their sexual peak until some time in their thirties. Because girls in their teens are just beginning to be awakened sexually and are in no big rush on their own account to have sexual intercourse, but often give in to their boyfriends' coaxing, they usually expect to be loved and cherished as a reward for having had sex. However, in most instances, the boy does not feel any special love for the girl after having sex. What he does feel instead is a tremendous relief. But there are other ways he can achieve that relief. There is no reason for you to "service" him—which is how a lot of girls feel about the experience, because there's so little in it for them.

## HOW DO GUYS FEEL THE DAY AFTER THE FIRST TIME THEY HAVE SEX WITH THEIR GIRLFRIENDS?

It may surprise you to hear how different a guy's reaction is to the experience of having sex. When asked what they felt after having sex with their girlfriends for the first time, most of them expressed joy and triumph, nothing like the anxiety and guilt that girls typically feel. Here's what the guys said:

I had no regrets. I was the happiest person on earth.
*Steven, 16*

I felt like I had finally reached the top of a mountain I had been climbing for a hundred years.
*Eddy, 19*

I felt different. Older. Much more mature.
*Michael, 16*

I didn't think there was anyone or any thing in the whole universe that could make me feel more happy, or ecstatic. But then there was a small part of me that said "What now?"
*King, 18*

It was great that I finally did something.
*Ray, 16*

I felt good about myself, like I accomplished something—especially since she played hard to get. I felt like a man.
*Bert, 18*

I was so shocked that she let me have her in that way. I felt like a million-dollar bill and then some.

*Antoine, 18*

I felt like I made a touchdown. I was smiling all the next day. Yeaaah!!

*Tom, 16*

The only reason I went out with her was for sex. Once I got it, I was satisifed and I didn't want to be around her.

*Bobby, 17*

I said, I finally achieved it. I finally got in her pants. But now that I think of it, I really wasn't considering her feelings at all. I was just looking to satisfy my needs.

*Jose, 17*

I felt shy and I didn't want to see her again or to look at her when we passed in the hall.

*Louis, 15*

Except for Louis, who was obviously embarrassed, the guys were happy—every one of them. And what were they so happy about? Unlike the girls, not one guy talked about being in love. Instead, they were quite pleased with themselves for having achieved a wonderful goal. In fact, one fellow even equates it with a touchdown in football.

For a guy, the sexual experience is a pleasure, a release, and what's more, a signal that they measure up as a male. Michael says he felt "more mature," and Ray really gives himself away by saying "I finally did something," while Bert comes right out and says that now he feels like a man. Cruder, more insensitive guys like Bobby and Jose admit that their only goal was sex (though in retrospect Jose realizes how selfish he was being).

Are these guys all shameless "cads," Don Juans who should be strung up by a female lynch mob? Did they plan to "use" their girlfriends? Of course not. They were simply following their biological urges. At least *they* got a physical thrill out of the deal, whereas most girls do not. But look at the language they use to describe their pleasure: Do you want to be some guy's mountain peak or touchdown, the means for him to prove he's a man, or the girl whose pants some guy finally got into? Wouldn't you rather wait and make love later, with someone older who already *knows* he's a man and respects you as a woman, instead of seeing you as something he's accomplished?

## THE DIFFERENCE BETWEEN WHAT SEX MEANS TO A GIRL AND A GUY

For many teenage boys, sex is a kind of proving ground, and the sex act is like "scoring" points in a game. It validates their budding manhood, reassuring them that they are indeed masculine. For a teenage girl, it's an act of giving, and in return for that gift, she expects an emotional commitment. But because the guy sometimes thinks it was all about "scoring" and has achieved his goal, he can walk away happy and guilt-free, not needing any further emotional contact.

The girl, on the other hand, is often left feeling used and unfulfilled. She has physically and psychologically opened herself, and what does she get in return for her "gift"? Rarely love, and certainly not orgasm. (It's very rare for teenage girls to experience full orgasm. Their bodies are simply not ready for that, and their boyfriends are too wrapped up in their own experience, and too unsophisticated, to be able to help them enjoy the act.) What she usually does experience is physical discomfort and emotional pain, a real feeling of betrayal. And in the bargain, sometimes she'll even have to endure the disrespect of the guy who now sees her in a different light, because she has fallen from grace in his eyes. "She should know better than that," he thinks. She's "too easy."

"It's not fair," you say, and you're right. But all too often that's the case. Let's explore this.

# WHY DO GUYS OFTEN DROP A GIRL SOON AFTER HAVING SEX WITH HER?

I asked guys if they had ever dropped a girlfriend shortly after having sex with her, and if so, why. Here's what they said:

You get bored. It's like a kid with a toy. When he first gets it, he spends all day with it. Then after he breaks it in, it's not fun any more, so he finds another toy.

*Reggie, 16*

It's just like in the meat market. You just want to go out there and get some fresh meat.

*Jim, 19*

Sometimes that's the way love goes when sex comes into it. The sex is good, but only for that day. After that, you're finished.

*Lewis, 16*

After I have sex with a girl, I don't care if I see her anymore.

*Jed, 15*

After the first time we had sex, we stopped talking. She never called me and I never called her. I thought she was an easy catch because she gave me sex too quickly.

*Winston, 15*

At first I really liked her, but after I had sex with her, I saw she wasn't all I thought she was.

*Antonio, 17*

I fooled around with this girl after I knew her for only a few weeks, in the summer. I didn't feel a closeness to her so I just dropped her.

*John, 16*

After we had sex, she turned bitter and our relationship was poisoned.

*Ivan, 18*

I stopped seeing her because after that, she thought she owned me, and I couldn't endure it.

*Lyron, 18*

After I had sex with my girl of four months, she started acting strange—kind of stupid, so I dropped her.

*Sean, 16*

It always happens too fast. I never waited a long time for sex. Sometimes I wish a girl would say no and keep saying no. If we took it slow, we'd probably still be together.

*Dean, 17*

Reggie, Jim, Lewis, and Jed make no secret of their feelings. To them, sex is for fun and pleasure only. Once they get bored with their new toys, their sex partner is just something to be thrown aside so that they can find an even newer one. I don't think this is what their girlfriends had in mind, do you?

Winston, Antonio, and John all lost respect for the girls they had sex with. They also seem to feel the sex occurred too early in the relationship. If so, then why did they approach the girls for sex in the first place? Like most boys, they tried, not only because they are physically "horny," but because they believe it is their obligation to try. That, unfortunately, is what society expects of young boys (as in "boys will be boys"). Yet, as Dean says, even when they're putting the moves on her, they're sometimes secretly hoping that the girl will slow things down. A guy never disrespects a girl for saying no. Yet guys often do lose respect for the girls who say yes.

The comments by Ivan, Lyron, and Sean highlight the problems that can arise due to the different emotional expectations that guys and girls have about sex. They all noticed that their girlfriends seemed somehow changed after sex, and this upset them. Ivan's girl turned bitter, Lyron's girl became possessive, and Sean's girl acted "strange." What they were noticing is easy for any woman to understand—the girls' need for an emotional and spiritual bond after sex, a need for closeness that these fellows apparently don't feel in themselves.

If all of this is true, imagine how a girl feels when a guy "drops" her shortly after having begun a sexual relationship? Well, you don't have to imagine—because I found a number of girls eager to share their experiences with other girls, in the hope that they could spare someone else the pain they went through.


## BEING DROPPED AFTER HAVING SEX— GIRLS TELL ALL

I asked girls whose boyfriends had dropped them shortly after sex with them to share their feelings with you. They said:

My boyfriend broke up with me three months after we had sex. I guess it was because there was no more suspense, nothing to think about, no more what-ifs. I felt horrible.
*Fran, 16*

I went out with a guy for a month and then had sex with him. After that he never called me again. I felt like a fool.
*Sunny, 16*

My boyfriend and I were alone in this place. We made love for the first time that day. It was really good. Three weeks later, he ended the relationship because he had another girl. I felt depressed about the fact that what we had that night didn't mean anything to him.
*Marva, 18*

My boyfriend and I had broken up, but he called and that night we made love for the first time. After that he said he "needed time to be alone." He was supposed to get back to me, but he never did. I felt used and betrayed. He had been my boyfriend for eleven months, and supposedly he loved me.
*Rochelle, 15*

Two days after I had sex with this guy he broke up with me. He said I was looking for a commitment and he wasn't. I wanted to kill him.

*Donna, 16*

A few days after I had sex with this guy he dropped me. I felt used.

*Connie, 16*

I went out with a guy for one week and had sex with him. After that, he wanted nothing to do with me. He dumped me. I guess he thought I was too much of a "quick lay." He didn't even think of me as a person. I was very disappointed because I thought sex was what he wanted from me—but it turned out not to be enough.

*Rosa, 17*

It was the second time I'd seen him since we met. The mood was there. He wanted to so I did it. But he didn't want to after that. I felt real easy and cheap, even though I'm really not. I just needed to be loved.

*Coco, 17*

Guys drop girls shortly after having sex for many reasons. Mostly it's because, as teenagers, they are simply not ready to settle down into a deep, emotional commitment, and they probably sense that if they continue the relationship, they'll be getting in deeper and deeper. Often they detect a new demanding, intense attitude in their girlfriends and realize that things are going to get too serious if they stay around—so they leave. The girl, of course, doesn't know what's going on in the guy's mind. She sees his leaving as a betrayal and feels used and angry. No matter how well you may understand intellectually what's going on, it's very difficult to detach yourself emotionally and say to yourself "Oh, I shouldn't take it personally. He didn't realize I would become so emotionally involved. I must remember that guys usually view sex differently than girls do." No. You may be able to offer those wise words of comfort to a friend whose boyfriend just left her after a sexual relationship, but when it happens to you, it's not that easy. It takes time to get over the pain. Time is a great healer, however, and if you learned from the experience, a great educator, too.

## IT'S NOT ALWAYS THE GUY WHO DROPS THE GIRL!!

In some cases, it's not the guy who drops the girl but the girl who drops the guy soon after having sex. Here's why.

I dropped him about a week after having sex because I despised him. He repulsed me because the sex was not based on love. He became a disgusting thought and sight. I didn't feel rejected but grossed out.

*Barb, 15*

After I had sex twice with him, it seemed he only wanted to hang out when no one would be home. After a while, we got in a fight because of his attitude and I broke up with him. I felt hurt and used but I still liked him, and I would have gone back, but I realized what he wanted me back for, so I said "No." Too bad I had to learn the hard way.

*Beth, 16*

I dropped him because I felt that sex was the main factor in our relationship. There was no respect or communication.

*Dawn, 16*

I knew he didn't really care for me, so I dropped him before he dropped me.

*Jasmin, 15*

The girls drop the guys because, basically, they're disappointed. The sex didn't turn out to be what they had dreamed it would be—and neither did the guys. No girl appreciates being ignored, picked on, taken for granted, or obviously "used" only for sex, which is how many girls in their teenage years end up feeling when they have sex. Girls expect an emotional commitment along with the physical connection, but they rarely get it.

## THE DANGERS OF TOO MUCH EMOTIONAL INVOLVEMENT—EVEN WHEN IT'S MUTUAL

There are some sensitive guys who do make that commitment once they have sex with a girl, but in the teen years, that is more the exception than the rule. Even when a commitment does develop, however, other trouble can arise. The girl and guy may become so emotionally entangled that they find it impossible to break apart—and often they end up getting married in their teen years. While some early marriages do work out, many fail for obvious reasons, among them, both partners need to explore, to develop and change, the discovery that their goals and values are incompatible, and, very commonly, two people blaming each other for being the cause of having to miss out on all the fun of their high school days. Also, marriage at an early age can hinder or stop both people's chances of having a good career, not *only* if, but especially if, a baby comes along. Before they know it, the financial responsibilities of adulthood are upon them, and there's little chance for college or professional training.

## LEARN, LEARN, LEARN

What should you do if you're in a situation where you're tempted to begin a sexual relationship with a guy? Think of it this way. Girls *don't* usually wake up in the morning and say "I made a terrible mistake. *I wish I had had sex with him last night.* I should have said 'yes.' " But many girls do wake up in the morning and say "I made a terrible mistake. I should *not* have had sex with him last night. I wish I had said 'no.' " If you say no, you'll always have a chance to change your mind later (because he'll still be trying to get you to do so). But if you say yes, a whole new relationship has begun—often a very short one, as both sexes would agree—and you can never turn it back to what it was before.

## HOW DOES SEX CHANGE A RELATIONSHIP? GIRLS' POINT OF VIEW

Even if sex does not end a relationship, it always changes it—but how? I asked girls to tell me what changes they had experienced after sleeping with their boyfriends. They said:

After sex you feel closer to your boyfriend—more attached to him. It's as if he knows everything about you now.

*Sarah, 16*

You have special ties—a bond. You've given yourself to him completely, shared your body with him, satisfied his needs. You think there will always be a commitment from him and are angry and hurt when you see there is none.

*Melissa, 17*

The feelings you have for someone you had sex with are different from someone you didn't have sex with, because now that guy has a part of you that you will never get back.

*Frieda, 15*

You feel like you have an empty space in your stomach when he's gone and you feel closely connected with him, even if you don't love him.

*Simone, 16*

He told me he loved me and he would never leave me. When we broke up I was going to commit suicide. I thought no other guy would ever go with me.

*Shannon, 17*

Sex is not just a physical thing. It involves emotions—
emotions that are hard to overcome once you break up.
You feel as if he used you if you break up.

*Beth, 16*

If you break up with a guy you didn't have sex with, so
what? You can walk away free. But if you break up with a
guy you did have sex with, it stays on your mind. You
worry over it in a haunting way.

*Jackie, 15*

The girls agree on one thing: Sex made them feel "connected" or bonded to their boyfriends. But that wasn't necessarily a good thing, as it turned out. After sex, there was
a tie, which, when broken, caused despair and emptiness
and often a feeling of being used. It even caused one girl to
think of suicide. Perhaps Jackie sums it up best: Sex brings
a lot of worry and anxiety to a relationship making it less
free and harder to walk away from. So to girls, sex is a
commitment of sorts, and even if the commitment turns out
to be one-way, the feelings have a long and often unhappy
life. You can't just walk away from them, even if you or
your boyfriend have walked away from the relationship.

## HOW DOES SEX CHANGE A RELATIONSHIP?
## GUYS' POINT OF VIEW

Do guys share the same feelings? Here's what they say:

The relationship immediately became more serious. We
started acting more like parents towards each other. I
found it harder to let her down when I wanted to break up.

*Nicky, 18*

She became attached to me and wanted to see me every
night and got hurt and upset when I didn't want to, so we
broke up. There were bad feelings on her part. I was glad
to get out of it.

*Dwayne, 18*

The girl falls too deeply in love with you and you don't want to see her anymore.

*Carmine, 16*

Everything got very serious after sex. No more fun.

*Cory, 17*

She acted as if I should worship her just because she was having sex with me. I got disgusted with her.

*Lucien, 19*

We felt more commited to each other and we started to argue a lot more.

*Fred, 15*

After we had sex I thought I could do anything I wanted, and she would just be there for me, I was wrong.

*Lionel, 17*

Sex either makes a relationship grow stronger or die— but usually the relationship dies because you're not ready for that much of a commitment.

*Paul, 17*

The guys are quite intuitive. They clearly see the change in the girl's attitude, and can feel her sense of "connectedness"—only most of the boys feel this new bond as a threat and seek to break it. Perhaps Paul expresses it best when he says that guys are usually just not ready for that level of commitment. Notice also that with the exception of Nicky, it doesn't seem to be harder for *a guy* to break up with a girl after sex has entered the picture. Sex is not only *not* an inducement for guys to stay in a relationship—its after-effects often cause them to want to get out, and as Dwayne said, to be glad about escaping.

Not fair, you say again. Well, the hard facts are, women in general, not just teenage girls, are usually more emotionally committed to a relationship once sex enters into it than guys are. Perhaps this is one of those genetically grounded instincts: Because the girl is the one who can become pregnant and bear a child, it makes sense that within her genetic makeup there would be the urge to hold onto the potential father of her child, the provider and protector. Although birth control and abortion, not to mention changes in the status of women, may make this instinct outmoded, our genes don't know that—so there you are, trying to hold on to somebody whose own instincts are leading him away.

## CAN A GIRL REMAIN A VIRGIN IN THE NINETIES?

What's a girl to do then? Let me say right up front that I'm all for abstinence. What ever happened to good old-fashioned "making out"? Kissing, hugging, cuddling, and so on, is fine for teenagers, but sexual intercourse is for adults. The fact is, nobody ever died from not having sex—but some people are dying from having it, thanks to a disease called AIDS. And even if you practice "safe sex," there's no such thing as emotionally safe sex. The stakes escalate once you have a sexual relationship with your boyfriend, and as you've just heard, neither sex deals with the resulting complications very well. So my advice is—wait.

## ONCE YOU'VE SAID YES, CAN YOU START SAYING NO?

But what if you've already had sex? Is there any point to saying no once you've lost your virginity? Does a girl have to keep having sex with future boyfriends once she's had sex in the past? Let's see what other teenage girls say.

Of course not. No one is going to hold a gun to your head and say "You have to do it with every boyfriend from now on." You have freedom of choice.

*Debra, 18*

No. There are some boys who think sex isn't everything. They feel there's more to life.

*Jennifer, 17*

No. Maybe the one you did it with was a mistake and now you've learned a lesson. Why make the same mistake twice?

*Randie, 16*

Sex is not just for pleasure. You should have a strong feeling for your partner and you should be able to trust him. I'd wait for the next time until I was sure.

*Patricia, 17*

No. Not with all the diseases going around.

*Diane, 15*

No, but I do believe that once you've had sex, it makes it more tempting to do it the next time if the guy pressures you. But all you have to do is remember the end result and you'll be able to say a loud, clear NO.

*Ruth-Ann, 16*

You might feel guilty—like you gave it to one boy so why not give it to the next one? But there's no reason to feel that way. Your body is yours and nobody has any claims on it.

*Caprice, 16*

No. As a matter of fact, I think you can wait until you're married, and then you will feel like a virgin, even if you're not one.

*Dana, 16*

No, because if you do, you're going to end up winning a trophy for the biggest fool.

*Shannon, 17*

No. That's a bad rut to get stuck in. You should only have sex with a boyfriend you are both physically attracted to *and* deeply in love with. Even then, it's like opening a can of worms. I wouldn't advise it.

*Simone, 16*

The girls are clearly in agreement. You don't have to continue having sex just because you have had it before. You have freedom of choice—even though it may be tempting to do it again because you know you're no longer a virgin. They advise you to think of what happened in the past as a lesson for future relationships. As Simone so aptly puts it, you may decide to have sex again with someone you love, but "even then it's like opening a can of worms." In other words, the same problems you experience the first time are likely to come up again, because of the differences in what teenage boys and girls expect of sex.

## GIRLS' ADVICE ON WHEN TO START HAVING SEX

Because I am a good deal older than you, and you may think I'm just too old-fashioned in my beliefs, let's see what your peers have to say about this subject. I asked girls to advise other teenage girls as to when they should begin a sexual relationship. They say:

Once you've lost your virginity, you can never get it back. Make sure you're in love—and then some.

*Tara, 15*

Wait. If he says he likes you so much, yet he just wants to get his own way, no matter how you feel, that stinks. But it happens all the time.

*Andrea, 18*

Wait until you're an adult because when you're a teen, you're vulnerable—easily hurt. At least if you're an adult, you know what you're doing.

*Marsha, 18*

87

It may be unrealistic, and I don't think it's a sin if you don't wait, but if you have sex in relationships when you're not married you're taking the risk of having a very painful breakup because of the sexual ties.

*Marthe, 16*

It sounds tacky, but I say wait until you're married. I know guys have more respect for virgins.

*Sally, 17*

Wait until you're married. Then when you have sex, it will mean something—that you're in love with your husband and want him to be the first.

*Raquel, 17*

There are a lot of guys who only want one thing, and after that, you're history. If you do it, make sure it's with the one you're going to spend the rest of your life with.

*Jennifer, 17*

A girl should wait until she's totally in love with someone. Just to have sex out of curiosity or what have you is a mistake. You'll never get the full effect that way. Don't lose your virginity for just anyone.

*Aminah, 17*

Guys are users and abusers. They just want to feed their pleasures and desires. They aren't concerned with your feelings at all. They just don't want to get blue. . . . So make sure sex is something *you* want before you have it.

*Shannon, 17*

Wait until you're sure you are ready. If you don't you'll find yourself living in a confused and scary state. If I could turn back the clock, I wouldn't have had sex yet.

*Frances, 16*

I say twenty-one is a perfect age. You're mature and you understand life.

*Electra, 16*

You should wait until at least twenty, because then if you get dumped by a guy you can cope with it. You're more mature. If I had it to do over again, I would save my virginity until I was married.

*Valerie, 18*

Sex is not a sport or a skill. It's an emotional/physical thing that can affect your whole life. Look before you leap. Make it a rule not to have sex until you're at least eighteen—and then, proceed with extreme caution.

*Jocylyn, 16*

You should at least finish high school first. Sex complicates things. If you get pregnant, you could end up on welfare—you and your baby in misery.

*Lena, 13*

Never do it because he's pressuring you. You have to be responsible for your own life. Don't give your body to a boy just because he says you turn him on so much he can't control himself. Too bad for him. It's your body. And where is he going to be when the baby is born?

*Robin, 17*

Some boys say "If you love me, you'll have sex with me," and some girls believe that if they do it, they will keep him. But having sex with a guy doesn't make him stay, because when he's ready to take off, believe me, he'll take off anyway.

*Judy, 14*

## A MINIMUM SEX AGE—LIKE A MIMINUM DRINKING AGE?

The girls agree on one thing: Sex isn't something to be taken lightly. All advise you to think very carefully before making the decision to have sex. As you might have guessed, I would agree with the girls who say "Wait until you're married." However, if you find that idea hard to accept, the idea of a "minimum age," as some girls suggest, is a good one. If you were to pick an age and vow to yourself that no matter what happens, no matter how tempted you are, no matter how much in love you are, you won't have sex until that age, you would at least have set some limits for yourself, given yourself a framework in which to operate. You'll feel good about the fact that you had the self-discipline to keep a promise to yourself. And again, this applies even if you've already had sex. Just because *you* know you've had sex doesn't mean anyone else needs to know—or to form any expectations on the basis of that knowledge. If you ex-boyfriend spreads rumors about you—remember, unless it's on video, he can't prove it.

Will you be missing out on anything? No. Not at all. Believe me, you have a whole lifetime ahead of you, and sex is sooo much more enjoyable when you're a full-fledged adult with a calm, clear mind and you know what you're doing.

## GUYS' ADVICE—TO GIRLS—ON WHEN TO START HAVING SEX

Hmmm. Ever wonder what the guys would say? You might think they would advise all girls to go out there and have lots of sex—this way they would have no trouble finding partners. But surprisingly, they don't. When they're giving advice to all girls, instead of trying to persuade one particular girl, they say:

Don't give it up too quickly. Wait until you're in love, and learn from your mistakes.

*Anthony, 17*

Don't pretend you like sex when you're not really into it. Also, watch out—if you do it, you might get a bad reputation.

*Mike, 16*

Wait until you're sure you won't feel hurt, used, or cheated. Really think about the intimacy of sex and if you do it, use birth control.

*Jeff, 17*

Wait until you're married. Young men today are looking for young women who have not been used, abused, and accused.

*Robert, 18*

Girls should wait until they're over eighteen. What's the rush? You'll get more out of a relationship if you wait. The worst mistake you can make is to give in just because I want it.

*Willie, 18*

I know girls won't listen to this unless they're dedicated, but I advise them to wait until they're married—but at least don't do it at an early age and let guys hit on you. They only go away thinking "Hey, I got laid."

*Joey, 17*

Wait until you're married. Most guys out there are users and you'll end up getting hurt, having a bad reputation, and, more than likely, in the long run, being alone. Don't do it to make your boyfriend happy.

*Hamilton, 18*

Think about your mistakes and use them in your decision with the next guy. In other words, don't do it until you're mature.

*Orlando, 17*

Don't give in to guys who just want to use you for oral sex. We talk about girls like that behind their backs. You should hear what we say.

*Brandon, 16*

You must learn how to say "Hell no." Wait until you're twenty-one, but if you don't wait, use protection. Don't rely on the "pull and pray" method.

*Reggie, 16*

Girls should wait until they know what they're doing, then no matter what, don't tell anyone else about it or other guys will expect the same treatment.

*Ronald, 16*

Make sure the guy is mature and that he won't tell his friends, and that he really loves you. If I was a girl, I would not give it up until I got married. You just can't trust these guys.

*Jeremy, 16*

Wait until you've been going out with the guy for a long time—and you know he's not just out for one thing.

*Les, 16*

Using sex to make guys like you is a big turn-off. Make very sure you have no doubt about the guy.

*Peter, 16*

When guys are being honest, they know it isn't good for a girl to start having sex at an early age. Some of them have learned from experience that it causes big problems for girls. How can they dare to say this when they are the ones who are always trying to get girls into bed? Welcome to the world of the double standard. It's probably been around for as long as men and women have been around, and even in the nineties, despite all the other things that may have changed because of the feminist movement, it's obviously still around. A guy will still try to have sex with a girl he's physically attracted to, but he will respect that girl more if she says no. He will still have sex with girls who say yes, even though he knows it isn't the best thing for them. As discussed at length in *The Opposite Sex Is Driving Me Crazy*, he thinks this way: "It's my job to try and it's her job to say no. If she says yes, my conscience is clear." Some guys do have more sensitivity when it comes to sex, of course, but not many. The best you can expect from most of them is some guilt—and how does that help you? So it looks as if you'll have to watch out for yourself and be the one to make your own intelligent decisions.

## REMINDERS

1. Girls and guys often have very different feelings the day after the first time they've had sex. Girls often have mixed emotions—at best. Guys are usually unreservedly happy.

2. Couples often break up soon after having sex—for a variety of reasons.

3. When a relationship ends after sex has become a part of it, girls often feel angry, disappointed, guilty, rejected, depressed, or regretful. Not so with most boys.

4. One thing that girls and guys agree on is that once sex enters a relationship, things change. The relationship becomes much more intense and "serious." This in itself can lead to a breakup.

5. Teenage girls and guys both advise that it's a good idea to think more than twice before entering a sexual relationship (although you won't hear that from a guy in the heat of the moment).

6. Teenage girls agree that it is possible to refrain from having sex with future boyfriends—even if you've already had sex with former boyfriends.

7. I'm from the "old school" when it comes to virginity. What ever happened to making out? Many teenage girls also advise virginity until marriage, but some suggest a "minimum age for sexual relationships," such as eighteen or twenty-one.

# 6

# Friends ... And Your Boyfriend!

Most people have friends, and those of us who are lucky have a best friend. What is a friend anyway? A friend is someone you can go to when you have a problem or a complaint, a person to whom you can tell your most intimate secrets—someone who will listen and understand, and take your side in a conflict. But a friend is also someone with whom you can let down your hair and just "hang out." You can do wild and crazy things with a friend and later look back and laugh about it. Nobody should be without a friend.

But friends often take a backseat once a girl has a boyfriend. Why is this? Is it possible to stay close with your friend even if you or she has a steady boyfriend? How does a guy feel about it when a girl drops all her friends for him?

Friends come in both sexes, or so they say. Is it really possible to keep a guy as a friend? What's the best way to handle it when a guy who's a friend starts falling in love with you? Is it possible to be friends with an ex-boyfriend?

Some difficult and embarrassing situations can arise when you're around your best friend and her boyfriend a lot. What's the best way to handle it if your best friend's boyfriend makes a pass at you? Should you tell her or keep it to yourself to avoid stirring up trouble? What would *you* do if you found yourself falling in love with your best friend's boyfriend? Would you tell her, or just avoid being around her when she's with him?

These and many other matters regarding friends of both sexes will be discussed in this chapter.

## DO GIRLS NEGLECT THEIR FRIENDS WHEN THEY HAVE A BOYFRIEND?

I asked girls to tell me honestly if they ignore their friends when they have a boyfriend. They say:

I do because I want to spend every spare moment with him. I figure there will always be time for my friends later. If I make plans with my friends and at the last minute my boyfriend is available, I would cancel the plans I had with my friends and make time for him.

*Phyllis, 16*

I do it because when they have boyfriends, they neglect me. We all agree that if our boyfriends came to see us when we're with each other, we'll leave to be with the guys.

*Peggy, 17*

Usually, when you go out with your friends, you're looking for a guy. Now that you have him, you want to spend time with him.

*Judy, 15*

Sometimes it happens unconsciously. You want to spend every minute with him, and you take your friends for granted, although you shouldn't.

*Bunny, 15*

I don't do it deliberately, but if I'm having this great relationship I get so busy with him that sometimes I don't even remember that I have friends.

*Dora, 16*

It's natural. When you're in love, he's the only thing on your mind. You don't get the same love from your friends that you can get from a guy.

*Eilene, 17*

Your boyfriend becomes your best friend, so he takes the place of your friend. Most of the time you want his love, sympathy, comfort, and companionship more than anyone else's.

*Elizabeth, 16*

He said he didn't like my friends, so I stopped being with them. Now I don't talk to him any more, and my friends are not speaking to me—because I used to be with him all the time and I didn't have time for anyone, not even myself or my family.

*Pam, 14*

All your attention is focused on him and nothing seems as important as him. But in truth, your friends in the end will always stick by you. Your boyfriend won't.

*Andrea, 18*

I never neglect my friends, because if I do, then who will be with me when my boyfriend and I break up?

*Barbara, 14*

Boyfriends come and go, but friends last forever.

*Dawn, 16*

You can laugh and joke with your friends and do anything with them, and when you have problems, they can help you get things off your mind—but a guy can't always do that for you. So I try to make time for my friends, even when I have a boyfriend.

*Roz, 13*

You have more things to tell your friends than your boyfriend. Hell, there are some things you just can't tell a boyfriend—you know what I mean.

*Rachelle, 14*

As you can see, most girls admit neglecting their friends for their boyfriends. Some girls take their friends for granted when they have a boyfriend because they feel that their boyfriend is a "rare commodity." Phyllis would cancel plans with friends even if her boyfriend called her at the last minute. Her attitude is "There will always be time for my friends." What does she think—that her boyfriend is going to disappear into thin air if she doesn't keep her eye on him every minute? And that, on the other hand, friends will be there for her no matter how she treats the friends? Where is it written that friends should be willing to take all kinds of insensitive and inconsiderate treatment? What Phyllis is really saying is that to her, a man is like a god who must be put first at all costs. But she's in for a big disappointment when she discovers that men are only human and that they don't appreciate being placed in that role. In fact, as you'll see later, it makes them nervous when a girl builds her entire life around them—and it makes most of them want to run. Phyllis may also be disappointed to discover that friends don't always stick around if you've abused them. Pam's didn't!

Peggy and her friends have an agreement that they'll put the guy first and drop each other whenever one of their boyfriends comes around. This is not surprising because in our society, women have been taught that men come first. (Men, by the way, are taught the opposite—women are to fit into their lives wherever it is convenient for them. And too often we do just that, as many of these girls have told you.)

Judy's attitude is about the worst of all. To her, a friend functions only as a convenient helper to meet guys. Once she's achieved that goal, she doesn't need a friend. Doesn't she need someone to hang out with and talk to and tell her secrets to? I guess not.

What happens to Bunny, Dora, and Eilene is natural—when they're really in love with their boyfriends, they forget their friends, although they don't mean to. As discussed in Chapter 4, when you're in love, you *do* want to spend every waking moment with your guy. In fact, as Elizabeth points out, the guy becomes, in a way, your friend—so you don't need to be with your friends as much.

*As much.* I think that's the key phrase. The truth is, when you have a boyfriend, you will naturally spend less time with your friends, because there are only twenty-four hours in a day. The obvious solution is to divide your time between them, not necessarily equally, but in whatever way is comfortable for you. If you don't set aside any time for friends, however, when you break up with your boyfriend, you may find, as Pam did, that your friends are gone, too— just when you need them most. It's important to remember, as do Andrea, Barbara, and Dawn, that boyfriends come and go, but friends, if you treat them right, can last forever.

In addition, as Roz and Rachelle say, no matter how great your relationship is with your boyfriend, there are certain things you just can't say to him and do with him. Friends cannot and should not be replaced by boyfriends. Instead, they should be woven into the whole fabric of your life. Keep a balance, and you won't regret it.

## HOW TO REACT IF YOUR FRIEND NEGLECTS YOU FOR HER BOYFRIEND

It's tempting to feel rejected and angry when this happens. But if you think about it, your friend is probably feeling the way some of the girls just quoted feel. She's so in love that she can't help wanting to spend every moment with her new love. I'm sure she thinks about you and misses you, but since her time is so limited, she wants to spend it all with him.

If this happens to you, you can either get angry with your friend and say nothing—just silently resent her—or you can bring things out in the open. You can have a heart-to-heart talk with her, telling her how much you miss her and how much you wish you could have those long talks you used to have. You can explain to her that you hope she can spare a little time for you so the two of you can still be "confidantes'' or soulmates, even if she's no longer available for things like going to the mall or going out to parties—the kinds of activities you used to do together to meet guys. Understandably, her boyfriend would probably object, so you'll have to find other friends to accompany you on those outings.

Don't feel bad if it's you (the one without a boyfriend at the moment) who has to make the first move to keep the friendship alive. What counts is that in the long run, you educate your friend so that she does not lose you because she foolishly thinks a boyfriend and a friend are an ''either/or'' proposition. You can help her to realize that now, more than ever, she needs you as a friend, because she's probably feeling a lot of new, deep emotions for her boyfriend that need ''talking out.''

## HOW DO GUYS FEEL WHEN A GIRL NEGLECTS HER FRIENDS FOR HIM?

Do guys like it when a girl drops all of her friends the moment she starts going out with them? Here's what they say:

In a way it makes me feel special, but sometimes you need time alone, without her, maybe to see your own friends, or something like that.

*Scott, 16*

After you've been with someone for a while, you're going to need your space, or you'll feel smothered. That's why girls should not neglect their friends.

*Joseph, 18*

Even though it makes me feel good to know I'm first in her life and affections, sometimes I just want to be left alone to think. Don't crowd me.

*Dave, 17*

I don't like it because it makes me feel like I'm all she's got. That's too much pressure.

*Tom, 15*

She should spend more time with her friends because I won't be around like they will.

*Lyren, 18*

It makes me feel special, yet when we're together too much, we end up fighting.

*Jimmy, 15*

Apparently, while most guys *are* flattered that their girlfriends put aside their friends for them, they're also uncomfortable when this happens. The fact that they use words like "smothered," "crowded," and "space" indicates that they feel invaded when a girl has nothing else to do with her time but spend it with them.

The answer is clear. As tempting as it may be, ladies, spend a little time away from your boyfriend with your friends. Sure—you'll miss him and probably think about him while you're with your friends, and you may even worry that he's flirting with other girls. That's normal. Missing him is great—and your absence will make *his* heart grow fonder, too. And as far as flirting with other girls, let's be realistic: You can't put a leash on him, can you? If he wants to go for another girl, he will. But more than likely, he'll miss you, too, and be thinking about you just the way you're thinking about him. Don't you like to look at other guys and flirt with them at the same time that you treasure in your mind the fact that you're going to be seeing your boyfriend later?

If you keep your friends and give your boyfriend space at the same time, you'll be upgrading the quality of your life in several ways. You won't be 110 percent dependent on your boyfriend, or a slave to his every whim, and he'll miss you more and appreciate your presence in his life to a greater extent. You'll also have achieved a healthy balance—friends who can give you perspective on your love life and the rest of life, and a boyfriend who values you all the more because you've maintained some independence from him.

## IS IT POSSIBLE TO HAVE MALE FRIENDS?

Have you ever heard the saying "There's no such thing as a platonic relationship"? This statement means that it's impossible for a girl and guy to just be friends. I totally disagree with it. Of course the interaction between male and female friends is different from that of same-sex friends. What's especially valuable about a female/male relationship is that the two friends have something unique to contribute to each other—the point of view of the opposite sex. The inside dope on what the other sex thinks about typical situations can be very helpful. Imagine being able to ask a guy about boyfriend trouble—what an opportunity! In addition, there's probably some chemistry between you—a slight physical attraction or a bit of flirtation, which is always flattering and even, it must be admitted, exciting.

Sometimes the attraction is stronger than other times, but mild flirtations between opposite sex friends are usually fun. They create just enough tension to keep things interesting. But what happens when a male friend begins to fall in love with you for real—and you just want to remain friends?

## WHAT TO DO WHEN A GUY WANTS TO BE MORE THAN JUST A FRIEND

I asked girls what they would do if this happened to them. They say:

I would sit down with him and explain that I don't have romantic feelings for him and that if he can't handle it, we'll be losing a great friendship. You have to nip that kind of situation in the bud before it gets out of hand.
*Marthe, 16*

I would tell him that our friendship means too much to me and I don't want to jeopardize it.

*Dawn, 16*

I would just tell him I am not the right one for him. You need to confront him and tell him that he cannot continue with these feelings.

*Sylvia, 17*

I would tell him that we've known each other a long time and he's like a big brother to me.

*Edith, 17*

I wouldn't say anything particular. My actions would show him.

*Estelle, 16*

I would give him the cold shoulder, talk mean to him. Then I would say, "I hope you don't think of me as more than a friend."

*Irene, 15*

I would avoid him completely.

*Lynn, 14*

If that's the way he feels, I can't do anything about it. As long as he doesn't get carried away, I'd ignore the situation.

*Terry, 18*

I'll tell him that I'm already taken and I don't love him enough to have an intimate relationship.

*Maria, 17*

Marthe, Dawn, and Sylvia would take the direct approach, telling the guy that they value his friendship, but making it clear that they want nothing more. While this may be painful for him to hear, because it's disappointing, it's a very gentle way of letting him down, and a real compliment to him as well. After all, they're not rejecting the guy completely—only as a potential boyfriend. In fact, they're confirming his value as a dear and treasured friend.

Edith uses a little psychology. By telling him he's like a big brother to her, she bolsters his ego, making him feel like a protector and advisor. But at the same time, she paints a clear picture for him—that of a brother-and-sister relationship. It then becomes much easier for him to rule out the idea of a romance. After all, who would think of his sister in a romantic way?

Estelle hopes that he picks up the message by her actions. But chances are he won't, if he hasn't already done so. If she goes a step further and, like Irene, gives him the "cold shoulder," he'll only become confused and angry. If she avoids the issue completely, as do Lynn and Terry, he will pursue her until she's forced to face it.

There's no need to hurt a guy's feelings the way Maria did. I'm sure she didn't mean to be cruel, but when she said: "I'm already taken, I don't love you enough to have an intimate relationship," her message was "You're not good enough for me." While this may be the way she feels, there's no reason to tell him so bluntly. It would only hurt him unnecessarily, and perhaps make it difficult for him to approach other women in the future.

All things considered, the best approach is the straight-forward one. Think of yourself. If you were in the situation, how would you like to be treated. Would you like to have the guy avoid you, give you the cold shoulder, tell you you're not attractive enough or sexy enough for him—or would you like him to tell you how much he enjoys your company, but that he's not interested in a romance?

## HOW CAN YOU BECOME FRIENDS WITH YOUR EX-BOYFRIEND—AND DO YOU WANT TO?

If you've followed the suggestions in Chapters 2 and 3, chances are, your ex-boyfriend will want to be your friend for life. He will have gotten used to the compliments, the comfort, the sympathy, the understanding, and the moral support that you've given him. He will have become addicted to your interest in his achievements and his personal life, and will miss the joy of talking to someone who shares his values. In short, he'll still be calling you for that "fix."

But what if you end up with five ex-boyfriends calling you up, who love you as a friend and want to remain your friend for life? Wonderful. Welcome them to the club. I have at least twelve, and I love it. And don't forget, friendship is never a one-way street—they'll be your friends, too. You can confide in them, laugh with them, cry on their shoulders, ask for favors and do them favors in turn.

I say, the more ex-boyfriends you can turn into friends, the better. But sometimes it takes awhile for an ex-boyfriend to become a friend—maybe a few months or even a year. Often, time is needed for the "dust to settle," so that the two of you can look at the relationship in perspective. More often, the one who did the walking is ready to be a friend first, because that person is not as emotionally "raw." But even the "walkee" (the one who was walked away from) can come around, in time.

There may be cases, however, where you feel you should "let sleeping dogs lie" and *not* develop a friendship with your ex-boyfriend. If this is the case, follow your instinct. You're probably right. Sometimes ex-boyfriends can be trouble—especially if there are still sparks between you, or your breakup caused a lot of hurt and pain for one or both of you. Let your inner being tell you what to do. So if an ex calls you and you think you can't handle it, by all means, cut it short.


## WHAT WOULD YOU DO IF YOUR BEST FRIEND'S BOYFRIEND MADE A PASS AT YOU?

This is a tough one. What would you do? If you tell your girlfriend, she may blame you or think you're the one who encouraged her boyfriend to flirt with you. If you don't tell her . . . well, let's see what the girls have to say:

I would tell her because he may be doing that with a lot of girls, and if it were my boyfriend, I'd want to know.

*Daisy, 15*

If he did it to me he would do it to another girl, and I would rather she heard it from me than from some stranger who might hurt her.

*Marla, 14*

I would tell because in case he tried anything on me and she found out, I wouldn't want her to say that I teased him.

*Miriam, 17*

He's a jerk and she should know what kind of guy she's getting involved with. If he asked me out, I have to make her aware that there will be others. He is trouble.

*Jessica, 15*

I would tell because sooner or later she's going to find out about what a double dealer he is when he does it to her other friends, and then she'll wonder why I didn't say anything.

*Joyce, 14*

I would tell her because I would want her to do the same for me.

*Cassandra, 16*

If I told her it would cause distrust and confusion, and she might think I was after her boyfriend. So I would just hang out with my friend, and be sure not to be around her when her boyfriend was.

*Tanya, 16*

I would keep it from her so it won't turn out to be a big situation.

*Karen, 18*

I would give the guy fair warning, but if he kept it up, I would tell. Then the rest is up to her.

*Babette, 17*

I wouldn't tell her—at least not right away. I would be afraid of her response.

*Ana, 16*

It really depends on how close I am with the friend and how far the flirting went. If we weren't that close, I wouldn't say anything, but if she was a good friend and the guy was making some heavy passes at me, I would definitely say something. She should know what a slime her boyfriend is, and I wouldn't want to see her get hurt by being played for a fool.

*Marthe, 16*

You can see the difference in personalities here. Some girls are the "totally loyal" type who would be so outraged that they would have to tell their friend immediately in order to save her further embarrassment—even if it meant being under suspicion themselves. Some girls, however, take a more analytical approach. They would wait it out and avoid the guy, or give him fair warning, in the hope that they would never have to confront their friend with the facts. They realize that they might be under suspicion, and probably feel that they couldn't cope with this, especially because they know they are innocent, so why stir up a hornet's nest?

What would you do? Knowing myself, I would have to tell and let the chips fall where they may. But you may choose to handle it differently. It's your decision, and it will always depend on the particular circumstances.

## FALLING IN LOVE WITH YOUR BEST FRIEND'S BOYFRIEND

Let's see what happens if the situation is reversed. What would you do if you were falling in love with your best friend's boyfriend? Girls advise:

I'd stay as far away from him as possible and try to forget he exists, keep my mind off him.

*Didi, 16*

I would stop thinking about him and not hang out with my friend when he's around.

*Franchesca, 15*

If the chemistry was there and we both knew it, I would talk to him about it.

*Tina, 17*

I would try to control myself. I'd act like nothing was different and not let either of them know what I was feeling.

*Rita, 13*

I'd tell my friend, even if I knew it would ruin our friendship.

*Delilah, 16*

Cut it short. As tempting as it may be, you can't backstab because it will only come back on you.

*Tracy, 18*

Most girls would handle it by trying to avoid the guy in the hope that the feeling would pass. This could happen, especially if, in the interim, another guy comes along to divert their attention. But what if that doesn't happen and the attraction becomes even more compelling?

Is it a good idea to talk to your friend about it? It's a big risk and a very tricky situation—which, as Delilah points out, could ruin the friendship.

The best course of action is to face the fact that you don't have to act upon every feeling you have. For example, when you see a delicious ice-cream cone, you don't have to buy it and eat it, do you? When you have an urge to punch someone in the nose, you don't have to haul off and let them have it. Of course not. You can control your actions. In the case of your friend's boyfriend, painful as it may be, the right thing to do is bite the bullet and let this one go—no matter what it takes. Otherwise, as Tracy says, who knows, one day it may happen to you. The tide always comes back. Think about it. What you put into life has a strange way of returning to you. It's a basic principle of life, I've found.

But what's more important, if you resist the temptation to do what you know you would never want done to you, you'll like yourself better. In other words, your "self-esteem" will rise. Your opinion of yourself will be more positive than had you taken the path of least resistance and gone after your friend's boyfriend. In the long run, high self-esteem is what you need to be happy and successful—but that's a whole other book.

## IS IT OKAY TO GO OUT WITH YOUR FRIEND'S EX-BOYFRIEND?

How would you like it if your best friend started going out with your ex-boyfriend? Here's what the girls say:

No way. That's not right. I just broke up with him and now I have to see him in my face all the time with my friend. Also, I would wonder if they had had feelings for each other all along.

*Tasha, 16*

Sorry. I can't deal with that. After all, there are so many pickings out there. Why does she have to scoop up the crumbs that fall from my table? I would be highly offended.

*Lauretta, 17*

If my friend went out with my ex I would resent it. How could she go with him when she knows I have history with that guy? No matter who did the breaking up, obviously there are still feelings. She can find someone else—or find another friend.

*Cleo, 14*

That happened to me and I didn't have it out with my friend until she stopped seeing him.

*Ro, 16*

If I broke up with him and couldn't stand him any more, then I wouldn't mind, but if he broke up with me and I still had anger toward him, then forget it.

*Gabrielle, 15*

I guess it would be okay if we were really finished with each other, and if we didn't have anything really deep together. But if I had this heavy thing with him, it would be hard to see them together.

*Lilly, 18*

The fact is, it's an uncomfortable situation no matter how you look at it. Because there are so many other choices, why pick up on your friend's ex? The answer is clear. Probably the two of you got to know each other while your friend was going out with him and, without realizing it, became attracted to each other. Maybe you slowly became aware of the fact that you two were even more compatible than your friend and he, but being loyal, you both suppressed your feelings until the time was right.

If this is your situation, I suggest a heart-to-heart talk with your friend. Be very open and honest. Chances are she'll appreciate your integrity and your respect for her feelings enough to give you the go-ahead, even if she wishes she didn't have to. It's hard to turn down someone who asks for what she could have just taken. If, however, she does say no, you'll have to think very seriously about what to do, taking into account whether you think your friend is being reasonable or not, and the depth of your feelings for her— and for her ex-boyfriend. Putting yourself in her shoes may help you to make a decision you'll feel right about later— and that does not necessarily mean obeying her wishes. There are no permanent property rights to ex-boyfriends.

## REMINDERS

1. It's natural to spend less time with your friends when you have a boyfriend, but don't neglect them com-

pletely. Although boyfriends have a special place in your life, they're no substitute for friends, who are likely to be around long after the boyfriend is gone—if you treat them right.

2. Guys are flattered when girls neglect their friends for them, but at the same time they feel threatened by this behavior. They respect and appreciate a girl who maintains her friendships while going out with them. In fact, showing a certain amount of independence usually enhances the relationship because, when guys know that they can't have all of your time, they'll value the time you do spend with them more highly.

3. Male friends hold a very special place in a girl's life, but when the chemistry is too strong, it's a good idea to bring things out in the open rather than avoid the issue.

4. You can be friends with your ex-boyfriends, but you'll have to decide whether or not the time is right.

5. When a best friend's boyfriend makes a pass, most girls would tell their friend. Others would keep it a secret in the hope of avoiding trouble. Each situation is unique and must be handled accordingly.

6. If you are falling in love with your best friend's boyfriend, the best thing to do is cut it off cold. There's no law that says you have to act on every feeling. If you resist the temptation, you'll feel better about yourself later. In the long run, self-esteem is more important than immediate gratification.

7. Don't go out with a close friend's ex-boyfriend until you've discussed the situation openly with her and explored her feelings.

8. Boyfriends come and go, but friendships last forever.

# 7

# Don't Play Hard to Get, Be Hard to Get

Isn't it amazing? It's always the guys you're not really that interested in who fall in love with you. Why is this true? There's a simple reason for it. When you don't really care for a guy, you don't jump at every chance to go out with him. You don't call him constantly, you don't sit by the phone and wait for his call, and you don't act eager and desperate when he does call. So what happens? The more you resist his advances, the more attracted to you he becomes. Why? Because you're hard to get. But are you *playing* hard to get? Of course not. You are *being* hard to get. It's for real. No game is involved. I'm not, of course, talking about being stuck up or hostile, the kind of activity I warned against in Chapter 2 in my discussion of how to meet someone you're interested in. It may seem to you that there's a fine line between being hard to get and playing dishonest games with a guy. But I think that you'll understand the difference by the end of this chapter.

Now if you could only be that hard to get with the guys you're crazy about, then they would pursue you, too. In this chapter you'll find out what to do in order to make sure you're *not* one of those girls who's always chasing, crying, complaining, pining, and whining about some guy. Instead, you're *being* chased because that's the only way a guy can get to you.

You'll learn what happens to relationships when a girl calls a guy too often, and you'll find out why it's not a good idea to demand that your boyfriend spend all his time with you. You'll discover how guys feel about girls who are always available and don't seem to have a life of their own, and you'll get advice from both girls and guys on how to be hard to get so that the guy you're interested in will be chasing you and not vice versa. You'll learn all of this, and much more, by observing the mistakes and triumphs of other teenagers.

## DO GUYS WANT GIRLS TO CALL
## EVERY NIGHT?

When you're in love with someone, it's tempting to try to talk to him every chance you get. I asked guys how they feel when a girl they like calls them every night. They say:

I don't like it because sometimes I feel like spending a quiet night alone without distractions of any kind. If she were to call on one of those nights, I'd probably act un-interested and break off the conversation fast.

*Joe, 17*

If a girl calls me every night, I would get tired of hearing her voice.

*Harv, 18*

I'm usually busy at night and I hate to have to stop what I'm doing to come to the phone. I'd rather call her, when I'm in the mood to talk.

*Bill, 19*

It's not good because although I do like her, I don't want to get tired of her. I feel more excited about a girl when I have to pursue her most of the time.

*Freddy, 16*

It makes me think she has nothing to do but call me every day. It also makes me feel as if she doesn't do anything but stay home.

*Martin, 18*

No. I would feel like she doesn't trust me.

*Richie, 19*

I would like hearing from her every night only if I don't see her during the day, and only if she's my girl.

*George, 15*

It's enough that I see her and call her on the weekend. I should be the one doing the calling.

*Chris, 17*

If I'm not going out with her, getting called every night makes me feel like I'm being smothered.

*Mike, 16*

I like girls who keep tabs on me.

*John, 16*

You want to know if they're still around, so I like it.

*Lewis, 16*

Guys seem to agree that they don't appreciate it when girls whom they're interested in, but not going out with, call them often. It turns them off because the mystery is gone. Obviously, guys enjoy pursuing girls, and don't appreciate being denied that opportunity. There is less agreement, however, on how they feel about being called regularly by a girl they are dating. Some guys view the constant calling as an invasion of their privacy, and their resentment is likely to surface in other areas of the relationship. They may pick arguments about minor things, for example, when what is really bothering them is the feeling that the girl is trying to take over their lives.

But other guys, like John and Lewis, for example, enjoy having a girl call them regularly. It makes them feel secure about the relationship. Such guys are in the minority, however, and if you're not sure of your guy, it's better to err in the direction of too few calls, which will only make him long for more, rather than too many, which can backfire—especially if you haven't even started dating.

In any case, it's a good idea to give him some space. Most people, not just boyfriends, would eventually become weary of you if you relentlessly pursued them. It's better to use a little self-control and resist calling him every time you get the urge. Remember, he has your telephone number, too!

Does this mean you should never call guy under any circumstances? Of course not. You can call your boyfriend from time to time, and you can even call a guy you just met, but there are some things to consider carefully.

Suppose you go out on a date with a new guy, and you have a wonderful time. You can't stop thinking about the guy. You think it's love at first sight or at least at first date. The next day you get the urge to call him and tell him what a great time you had. At first you hesitate to call, but then you think "Just because I'm a woman, why should I sit passively by and wait for him to call me?" Well, of course you can call him. In fact, he may be happy to hear from you.

On the other hand, you do run a risk by calling him first, and so quickly. Unfortunately, even though this is the nineties, some things are changing rather slowly. I've interviewed hundreds, even thousands, of teenage guys, and most of them feel more comfortable in the role of "pursuer rather than in the role of "pursued." If you call the guy the day after the first date, you take away his opportunity to pursue you. You also deny him the chance to worry about whether or not you care for him. In fact, you remove the mystery from the relationship, and much of the initial stages of falling in love involves the fear that the other person might not feel the same way that you do. It's better to let him stew a bit, don't you think?

Why not give him a chance to call first—at least a few days, and maybe even a week. Then you can certainly call him. If he hasn't called by then, who knows, maybe he lost your number or got into an accident or some such thing.

Generally speaking, the best idea is to use restraint when it comes to calling a guy. As difficult as it may be, I say let him do the calling. The next time you're tempted to pick up the phone when you know you shouldn't, say to yourself "He knows my number" and put it down. But . . .

## SHOULD GIRLS WAIT BY THE TELEPHONE WHEN A GUY SAYS HE WILL CALL?

Of course not. Go on about your business. If you're not home, he'll call you back. If the line is busy (and you don't have call waiting), he'll call you back. If you're out shopping or with friends, he'll call you back. Why wouldn't he? What makes you think that if you miss that one call, it's all over—you'll have no other chance? This is an irrational idea rooted in insecurity.

Although it's perfectly normal to have feelings of insecurity—most people do—you don't have to let them rule you. Once you think through your situation logically, you can break emotion's hold on you. Finally you will no longer be in the position of waiting by the phone, your heart soaring to the heights in hope whenever it rings, dropping to the depths when it's not his voice you hear when you pick up the receiver. Here's how to guide yourself into a healthier mental state. Whenever you're tempted to sit by the phone and obsess, you can instead think this way: I am a worthy and lovable person whether or not this guys calls me. Evidently he is interested in me or he wouldn't have asked for my number in the first place. He's probably just as eager to talk to me as I am to him—and just as worried about being rejected by me as I am about being rejected by him. In addition, there are many other guys out there who would love to get to know me—so there's no reason to place so much stock in this one phone call. Even if this guy never calls, or if I miss his call and he never calls back (which rarely if ever happens)—so what? Will the world end? Does it mean I'll never have a relationship with another guy? Of course not. It just means not having a relationship with someone whose interest in me was so slight he was willing to make only one call.

Learn to calm yourself down and think rationally. Remember, you are in control.

## HOPE AND DOUBT—
## THE MAGICAL COMBINATION

Once a guy calls, there's no reason to let him know how eagerly you were awaiting his call. Saying things like "I thought you'd never call," or confessing things like "I was thinking about you all day and all I cared about was getting home to receive your call," even if he just told you he's really attracted to you, is a *big* mistake. If he says complimentary things to you, wonderful. Let him talk. Let him be the one telling you how much you've been on his mind rather than vice versa. Be warm and receptive to anything he says along those lines, but don't be the one to initiate such remarks. You can let him know how much you enjoy hearing these things without going so far as to make similar statements to him. As far as how you feel about him, give him something to go on, but not too much. Give him hope but make him doubt at the same time. This magical combination results in passion. He'll be drawn to you, maybe even a little obsessed by the thought of you.

Another good idea is not to be home every single time he calls you. If you become too predictable and available, you'll interfere with the developing desire he has for you. You have to keep him a little worried, especially in the beginning stages of the romance. Anyway, keeping busy is one way of making sure you don't become obsessed with *him*. The more you can distract yourself, the more attractive and interesting you'll be to him, and the more you'll enjoy yourself, too. So make sure you keep having a life outside of your time with him.

Now let's talk about the time you do spend together.

# SHOULD YOU INSIST THAT YOUR BOYFRIEND SPEND EVERY WEEKEND NIGHT WITH YOU?

When you like someone a lot, naturally, you want to be around that person all the time—or do you? And even if that is what you want, is it a good idea? I asked girls if they think it's wise to demand that their boyfriends spend every weekend night with them. They said:

Give him his freedom. If you demand that he spend time with you, he'll feel smothered and pushed in the relationship.

*Jessica, 15*

You would get tired of him and he would resent you, too.

*Ann, 19*

Guys need time with their friends. If a girl is too demanding, the relationship starts falling apart.

*Susan, 15*

Guys get tired of girls who take up all their time very quickly. Also they want to hide from them and lie to them more often.

*Pat, 16*

Who wants to baby-sit a grown person? We both need to let each other do things by ourselves or we will resent each other.

*Tanya, 16*

If you're together every minute, a guy becomes frustrated and tired of seeing you and the relationship ends.

*Cindy, 14*

You don't ask a guy to spend all his time with you—you let it happen naturally. If you're both falling in love, then you'll both want to spend a lot of time together. But let him set the pace so you don't look too eager. If you whine about your boyfriend spending time with his friends, he'll think of you as a nag and probably break up with you. Let him take the lead.

*Marthe, 16*

Guys need time with their friends. Sometimes they just like to have fun together. If you are pressuring him and he wants to be with his friends, compromise. In other words, "Let him."

*Dixie, 16*

The girls are correct, but I wonder if all of them follow their own advice. Why is it that girls, and later women, so often find ourselves in the position of being the "nag" when it comes to spending time with guys? Most of us put ourselves in that position. We make the mistake of building our lives around a man, instead of pursuing our own goals and having our own friends. We imagine that the moment our "man" is out of our sight, he's flirting with other women. For example, if your boyfriend says he wants to hang out with his friends, I'll bet you picture him with the guys, walking through the mall and trying to pick up girls. In fact, however, guys usually have better things to do when they're with each other than cheating on their girlfriends. They have things to say to each other and activities to share that have nothing to do with girls, because even when guys do have girlfriends whom they care for, they continue to have other interests as well.

So take a lesson from your boyfriend's example. He's willing and ready to go out with his friends and have a good time. He evidently realizes that there's more to life than just a girlfriend. Notice, he's not building his life around you. And you shouldn't be building your life around him either. That's the biggest mistake many women make. Don't you do it. If you build your life around a guy, naturally you'll resent it when you find out that he's not doing the same for you—and rest assured, he won't. Don't make your "man," the center of your life. Instead, take an interest in all the other things that make for a full life: your schoolwork, friends, working out, school clubs, sports, community work, a part-time job, and so on.

What's more, when your boyfriend goes out with his friends, make a special point of not sitting at home and pining away for him. Go out yourself. Hang out with your friends or even your ex-boyfriend if he's turned into a friend. Go to a dance or a party or a club. Do something—whatever you want to do.

And don't, whatever you do, *don't* do what you want to do *only* when your boyfriend is busy with his friends. Go out without him from time to time. Have a life of your own.

## HOW DOES A GUY FEEL WHEN A GIRL IS ALWAYS AVAILABLE?

Do guys appreciate it when a girl jumps every time he snaps his fingers and comes when he calls? Let's see what they say.

That makes me less attracted to her, because what do I need with a girl who I can control and make do anything I want? If I wanted a pet, I would buy a dog.

*Mark, 19*

A girl should have her own thoughts and make her own decisions. If a girl acted like this, I would not respect her. After all, a girlfriend is not a slave.

*Todd, 15*

I'd hate it. That makes me feel she can't think on her own. She should have more pride in herself than that. It would turn me off.

*Curt, 18*

I would quickly leave her because there's no challenge and no variety in a relationship like that.

*Jeff, 17*

I totally don't like it. I hate girls who kiss up to their boyfriends. It makes me feel bad when a girl behaves in an inferior way.

*Orlando, 17*

I like a girl who has a life besides me—a girl with a mind of her own. It would make me nervous if she did everything I said.

*Andy, 16*

I want a girl to be my equal. I don't want to be like a father to her. She should have her own feelings and opinions.

*Seth, 16*

It seems clear that guys don't respect girls who are totally compliant. Instead, they appreciate and are attracted to girls who think for themselves and are willing to stand up for themselves when the situation calls for it.

The goal is clear. Don't be "easy" to get—too available, too agreeable, too willing to give up your own priorities and interests in favor of his. Let's see what teenage girls and guys have to say on this subject. First the girls, then the guys.

## GIRLS' ADVICE ON BEING HARD TO GET

Don't hang on his every word. The thing guys like best is a challenge, whether they admit it or not.

*Joanne, 16*

Act like the guy is not as important to you as he really is—like you're doing him a favor by going out with him.

*Marketa, 15*

Never let them see you sweat!

*Cassandra, 16*

Be cool but not bitchy. Don't make yourself too available.

*Misha, 14*

When he tells you he will call you, don't be there. When he asks, tell him something came up, but don't tell him what. When he asks you to call him at a certain time, don't call exactly on time, and then not on that day. Let him be hungry for you when you call.

*Kimmie, 18*

Don't always be available every weekend. Say you have to go somewhere, but don't tell him where. Leave a little mystery.

*Dawn, 16*

Let him give. Don't you always be the giver. It's okay to give once in a while, so long as he does too, but don't be a sucker. Let him respect you.

*Maureen, 15*

Flirt with other guys in front of them and talk about your past boyfriends.

*Jessica, 15*

Let him come and pick you up when you go out—don't meet him somewhere. When you go out, let him pay. Don't spoil him. That's the worst mistake you can make.

*Ruby, 18*

Beat around the bush when he asks you personal questions, even if you can and want to answer them. Let him worry.

*Celeste, 17*

Don't go out with a guy the first time he asks you out. Make him ask you out a lot of times, then just when he says "This is the last time I'm asking you out," say yes.

*Cher, 13*

Let's take a closer look at what the girls advise. Joanne, Marketa, and Cassandra advise that you not let him know how important he is to you. This is a very good idea, especially in the beginning. If you declare your feelings too soon in a relationship, it can make a guy stop going in the direction he's going in—trying to win you over. He'll know he already has you, and suddenly you'll find yourself chasing after him. Not a good position to be in.

Misha, Kimmie, and Dawn suggest keeping the guy off base by not always being available. I agree. By not always calling him when he's expecting your call, or not always being there when you're expecting his call, you make yourself all the more desirable, and him all the more uncertain about your feelings. And by not always saying yes to a date, you "keep him hungry," as Kimmie expresses it.

You don't believe it? Think of it this way. How do you feel about a guy who is totally predictable, who calls you every day, exactly when he says he will, and who is always available whenever you want to see him? You're sure of him—perhaps too sure—and you probably take him for granted. Before long, your heart doesn't beat fast when he calls. You say, "Oh, him again." And you may even drop him soon. But think of the reverse. Doesn't your blood rush when a guy who keeps you on edge calls? "How can I make this guy fall in love with me?" you wonder. "What can I do to win him over?"

Maureen warns not to be the "giver." She's probably referring to mothering—don't let him dump all his problems on you. She's right in a sense. Every relationship has to have a certain amount of give and take. You can do a lot of giving in the beginning, when you're using psychology, as discussed in Chapter 3, in order to get him hooked on you. But after a while, he should be taking a lively interest in you too—being concerned with your goals, interests, achievements, and sorrows. If not, it's time not just to withhold some of your generous impulses, but to reconsider the relationship and what you're getting out of it.

Jessica's idea about flaunting your relationships with other guys is *not* a good one, in my opinion. If you flirt with other guys openly, he'll feel obligated to defend his masculinity and he may start a fight with the guy or become nasty to you. At the very least he's likely to pay you back in kind. It's not worth it. Teenage guys' egos are too fragile for that sort of thing, and anything more than a bright, friendly smile to another guy would be out of bounds.

I agree with Ruby about letting him spoil you rather than vice versa. Let him pick you up. Except for special occasions, let him pay. In short, make him treat you like a lady. If you're fool enough to take over the role of the guy by paying and picking him up, human nature will take over and before long he'll lie back and let you do the work. I'm not saying that you shouldn't go dutch treat once in a while—especially if the two of you are seeing a lot of each other. After all, he's in school just the way you are. Still, men need special roles to play as men. That's why I think letting guys open doors for you, car doors included, is a good idea. If you take all of the male roles away from them, guys become confused. They may not tell you, but they really don't like it. Oh, they may let you take over out of laziness or weakness, but in the end, you're the loser. And in addition, you'll end up resenting him.

Celeste's got the right idea about leaving a little mystery about yourself. The worst thing a girl could do, for example, would be to discuss her romantic or sexual past with her boyfriend. No matter how hard he grills you, and how tempted you are to "tell all," don't do it. It's *always* a mistake. If you're in the mood for true confessions, go to a priest or a rabbi—or bite your tongue. If you start talking, believe me, you'll speak out of turn and you'll regret it later, because while guys are curious to know every detail about your past sex life, once you tell them, they will never forget it and they will hold it against you in their mind. Guys cannot handle anything related to your relationships with other guys, especially if it's sexual. Keep your mouth shut. Talk to your girlfriends, not your boyfriend.

Cher's idea about turning the first few dates down would be a good one, except for one problem: Teenage guys are very sensitive to rejection, and if you turn them down too often, they'll probably believe you really don't like them and give up. If you're a strong believer in playing (as well as being) hard to get, the best plan is to say you're busy the first time he asks you, but make it clear that you'd love to go out with him some other night. You might even suggest an alternate time. You may want to repeat this technique the next time he calls, or you could vary it by telling him that you have tentative plans to do something else for the night he suggests so you'll have to get back to him. Then make him wait a few days for your answer—let him sweat it out. This will force him to think about you as someone with a lot going on in her life, someone he'll be very lucky to be able to see. When you do finally say yes, he'll be much more thrilled than if you had said yes immediately. Don't feel as if you have to follow this advice. It's just an idea—a very old-fashioned one—but it seems to work wonders.

## GUYS TALK ABOUT GIRLS WHO ARE HARD TO GET

I asked guys to give girls advice on how to be just enough of a challenge to them that they don't give up. Here's the inside story on getting and keeping their interest, so pay strict attention, because they don't usually give away their secrets.

Show you're interested a little bit, then back away a little bit. It's like fishing. Let them keep nibbling at the bait, because soon they'll take the hook.

*Scott, 16*

Show a guy that you like him, a little, but keep him guessing.

*Rick, 15*

Don't pay as much attention as you would normally.

*Pierre, 16*

Don't act like you really, totally want to be with him. Make him work for your undivided attention.

*Lance, 17*

Just take it slow. Use your mind, not your feelings.

*Joseph, 18*

Keep the flame burning, but never too high. If you love him, only hint at it. Never come out and say it.

*Kyle, 19*

Don't act stuck up. Talk to him and get his phone number but don't give him yours, and then don't call him. He'll have to wait until he sees you to find out why. Then give a lame excuse, but do it nicely so that he'll still hold an interest in you. Then promise to call again and don't. If a guy really likes you, this will arouse his curiosity and make him chase you harder. When you do call, don't talk long, only about five minutes. This way he'll never really have a chance to find out anything about you and he'll keep chasing you. If you play your cards right, he may just fall in love with you, and that's when you can open up to him.

*Hamilton, 18*

Tell him how you really feel, then give him the cold shoulder. Be nice, then a little nasty at times, and always give him mysterious looks.

*Weston, 15*

Tease, but stay innocent. Don't have sex with him.

*Matt, 17*

Let's analyze what the guys are saying. Scott, Rick, Pierre, and Lance obviously speak from personal experience. Evidently, when they had to work for a particular girl's attention, she became much more valuable to them—a coveted prize, one worth waiting for and fighting for. Joseph and Kyle suggest using your mind instead of your emotions, and Kyle wisely adds that a girl should refrain from saying "I love you" to a guy before he's revealed his feelings. Most guys feel threatened when a girl declares her love, especially if they are not yet sure of how they feel. A guy may be well on his way to falling in love with you, but if you start spouting declarations of love, he will usually draw back because he'll feel things are happening too fast. There's no reason to tell all to a guy. You can think whatever you want to about him in the privacy of your own mind, but why does he have to know? It might just scare him away, and it'll definitely deprive you of the pleasure of hearing him say those words first. So don't rush in. That's the whole point of using your mind rather than your emotions—self-restraint.

Hamilton and Weston suggest torturing the guys with teasing behavior. I think they have a great idea, because the kind of teasing they're suggesting is not really negative or destructive, and guys evidently love it—while at the same time, of course, they hate it. This kind of torture can result in a guy's becoming obsessed with you, so if you've got the patience and the devilment to do it, why not try it?

Matt believes that not having sex is the best way to play hard to get. In a way he's right. One thing is for sure: If a guy is very attracted to a girl—her personality as well as her looks—and she does not have sex with him, he will see her as "hard to get" and will continue to pursue her. At first the pursuit may just be sexual, but eventually he'll be pursuing her because he knows that some one with such high standards is really special, and he'll be intrigued by that specialness. If that same girl, however, had had sex with him, possibly, for reasons discussed in Chapter 5, the relationship would have ended sooner than either might have hoped.

## BEING AUTHENTICALLY HARD TO GET

The bottom line on being hard to get is self-esteem or, if you will, knowing who you are. If you realize that you have a life of your own, with or without a boyfriend, that you are a worthy person, that you don't have to latch on to the first guy who takes an interest in you, that if things don't work out with this guy, there is no reason to believe that other guys won't be interested in you, you won't have to fake being hard to get, because you'll be genuinely busy leading your life. You'll still have plenty of time for guys, you just won't *always* have time for them. I'll have lots more to say on this in the last chapter, because this theme of self-esteem is extremely important.

## REMINDERS

1. When a girl calls a guy too often, most guys begin to resent the girl and/or become bored with the relationship. In general, it's better to let him do the calling. Guys like to think they're the ones who catch the girls— not vice versa. So let him think he's doing the chasing, even if you're active behind the scenes.
2. If a guy tells you he'll call, it isn't a good idea to wait by the telephone. Go on about your business. Believe it or not, he will call back if you're not there. Why wouldn't he? After all, he was interested enough to make the effort in the first place. And if he doesn't, so what? There will be plenty of others.
3. It isn't a good idea to demand that your boyfriend forsake his friends and spend every weekend night with you. In fact, you should regularly do things with other people. Make *yourself* scarce. Why should *he* be the rare commodity?
4. Guys don't respect girls who are "always available" and who jump every time they snap their fingers. In short, guys value girls who have a mind and a life of their own.
5. Both girls and guys advise that girls hold back when it comes to speaking out on feelings in the beginning of a relationship. Saying too much, too soon, can ruin everything.
6. The best way to *play* hard to get is to place a high value on yourself and actually *be* hard to get. If you do that, it's inevitable that guys will think of their time with you as something to be treasured.

# 8

# What to Do
# About Cheating

Cheating. You can't stand the idea of his cheating on you,
but if you innocently found yourself sort of cheating on
him, well, that's different. You believe in your heart that
cheating is 100 percent wrong, but then again, under certain
circumstances . . . You don't want to make an agreement
that it's okay for both of you to see others once in a while,
especially because you couldn't stand the idea of him going
with another girl, yet you wish you could do it and not be
considered a cheat.

The cheating dilemma—what can you do about it? Do
most girls cheat on their boyfriends, and if so, under what
circumstances? Do most guys cheat on their girlfriends? If
so, when and why? Would you break up with your boyfriend immediately if you found out he'd cheated on you?
Would most guys break up with their girlfriends if they
found out that she had cheated?

These and many other matters related to cheating will be
discussed in this chapter.

## WHAT IS CHEATING ANYWAY?

According to the dictionary, cheating means deceiving or
deliberately leading astray with the purpose of fraud. In

other words, the technical definition of cheating is "double dealing" with clear intent. You'll see later why this definition gets tricky when you try to apply the word "cheating" to teen relationships.

## Girls' Definitions of Cheating

I asked girls to give me their definition of cheating. They say:

Fooling around and falling in love with one person while you're still going with another.

*Marthe, 16*

Kissing or making out with a guy who isn't your boyfriend.

*Jennifer, 16*

Even going on a date is cheating if you have a steady boyfriend.

*Janice, 15*

Having a boyfriend and going out with someone else a few times.

*Debbie, 16*

If you're married and having an affair with someone else, that's cheating. Anything else does not apply.

*Sally, 17*

When your boyfriend is faithful and you're not.

*Charleen, 14*

Going out with and getting involved with someone when you still have the first guy on the line.

*Janie, 13*

Being in love with your boyfriend and sleeping with another guy on the side.

*Nita, 18*

Notice the wide variety of definitions—all the way from going out on a simple date with someone to "anything goes" unless you're married. Jennifer thinks kissing another guy is cheating, while Nita believes it's cheating only if you have sex with the other guy. Marthe skips all the physical details and says it's cheating only if you start loving another person. Charlene takes a different view altogether, stating that it's cheating only if *he's not* cheating on you.

But it's Janie's definition that's most commonly accepted: "Going out with someone new when you still have the first guy on the line." What's your definition? Never mind. Wait until you finish reading this chapter, you may change your opinion by then.

## Guys' Definitions of Cheating

Cheating is when you're fooling around with other girls besides your girlfriend.

*Scott, 16*

When you're going out with a girl for more than a month, and you start seeing another girl.

*Guy, 18*

Going out with two persons at the same time.

*Daniel, 17*

Having sex with a girl other than your girlfriend.

*Mickey, 16*

When you're in love with one girl, and you go out with another girl, and you feel guilty, you know you cheated.

*Joey, 19*

When you have made a commitment to a girl and go out with another behind her back.

*Vincent, 17*

Going with one girl and starting to see another girl while you're still going with the first one.

*Steve, 14*

130

Basically, guys are similar to girls in their ideas about what constitutes cheating—everything from actually having sex to kissing, or even just seeing one girl for a date while going steady with another. Now that we have an idea of what "cheating" means to teenagers, let's find out what rules they have for when it is and is not okay to do it.

## UNDER WHAT CIRCUMSTANCES IS IT OKAY TO CHEAT?

### Girls' Opinions

As it seems clear that cheating is not a clear-cut situation, I asked girls to tell me under what circumstances, if any, they think it's okay to cheat, and to give examples from their own lives. They had plenty to say:

When a person cheats on you, then you must cheat on him in order to feel less victimized.

*Ro, 17*

If you think your boyfriend is cheating on you, then by all means do it to him. I cheated on guy A with guy B, and then I cheated on guy B with guy C.

*Linda, 16*

It's okay to cheat when the circumstances are that your boyfriend could never find out, and you just feel like it. When I was in the Bahamas I kissed this guy I met in the disco, even though I was going with someone back home.

*Jennifer, 16*

If your relationship is going downhill, if it isn't fun anymore, then cheating is a good way of finding someone new. My old boyfriend was so unromantic he wouldn't even put his arm around me in the movies. So when I met a new guy who wanted to go out with me, I was curious, and sure enough, he was sweet, and I'm glad I did it. I ended up with him.

*Debbie, 16*

When the first guy is not around that much and doesn't have time for you, or you don't really like him anymore, then maybe it's time to cheat. When Jimmy was away, and Timmy and I were playing around, suddenly we started making out. He was sooo cute, I just couldn't resist. Afterward I said to myself, "I'm glad I cheated."

*Didi, 17*

If you feel you need to meet new people, or maybe your boyfriend takes you for granted—that's the time to cheat. I cheated on my boyfriend when I was working, and I don't regret it at all.

*Ada, 18*

Do it any time you feel like it. You're young, you're not married, so why not?

*Becky, 15*

There's full agreement on one point—all the girls think it's perfectly okay to cheat if the guy is cheating on you. Most girls seem to think it's okay to cheat if the relationship is already in trouble—if they feel taken for granted, or bored. Others feel that cheating on a vacation is all right, because no one will suffer. Still others feel that as long as you're not married, anything goes. What do the guys feel?

## Guys' Opinions

Cheating is wrong under any circumstances. I did it only once. When I was going out with one girl, I met another girl at a party and started making out with her.

*Richie, 19*

If the two girls live far away from each other, it's okay. I cheat on my girl all the time, except when I'm near her house or when her friends are around. I was messing around with this girl in the Bronx and with a girl in Manhattan at the same time. No harm ever came of it.

*Freddy, 15*

When you're getting tired of seeing that same face, then I think it's time to cheat. I used to send my girl home early because another girl was coming to my house.

*Joey, 19*

It's okay if you're on vacation and you're swept off your feet. When I went to L.A. I met this girl in the pool and we were swimming and having fun for three hours. It happened so fast, before you know it we were kissing and it felt like we loved each other. I told her "This is crazy. I have a girl back home that I love." But we spent most of the vacation together.

*James, 17*

It's okay to cheat when you meet someone you really like. You have to check her out or you'll always wonder what you're missing. I did this when I was fifteen but I stayed with my girlfriend in the long run.

*Darryl, 17*

If you're getting bored with your girl, as long as you tell the other girl you have a girl, it's okay. I did this and it was a perfect setup.

*Errol, 18*

Notice that guys don't even mention the idea of girls cheating on them. They may worry about this, but they won't admit openly that their girl could possibly be cheating on them. Is this wishful thinking or a way of protecting their "machismo"?

Guys agree with the girls that cheating is okay once the relationship gets boring, and most guys seem to feel that there's nothing wrong with checking out a new possibility. Like the girls, they feel that they're only young once and would not condemn themselves if romance just "happened spontaneously," as it did to James in L.A.

Cheating seems to be a universal phenomenon among teenagers. Even virtuous Richie, who says cheating is wrong under any circumstances, admits that he cheated when one thing led to another at a party.

Why do teenagers cheat? Maybe it has to do with the way teenage relationships have changed. In the fifties most teenagers dated more than one person at a time—openly. But couples didn't become as emotionally involved as young teens do today, and they usually didn't have sex. In addition, when teens did "go steady," they would break up much more quickly than teens today, so the need to cheat was minimized. When the steady relationship lasted a long time, it usually led to an engagement, which led to an early marriage—as soon as they graduated high school. In fact, in those days early marriage was encouraged. Perhaps that's part of the reason more teens were willing to wait to have sex. They knew that it wouldn't be that long before they would have a regular sexual partner, and they didn't mind saving themselves for that day in the not-too-distant future.

Today things have changed. Perhaps because of the media, teens are becoming more intense in their romantic relationships, modeling them after the affairs between adults that they see depicted on every TV and movie screen. They expect more from each other, and sooner.

But there's another reason teenage relationships have changed and become more complicated, and that is sex. As discussed before, once sex enters the relationship, emotions become highly charged. Guys become overly protective (if they are in love) and girls become overly possessive. It isn't easy to be dating more than one guy when you're having sex with one of them—even if you're not having sex with the others. You feel a lot more guilty about seeing others—almost the way you would if you were married and dating another man on the side but not having sex with him. And imagine the complications and guilt if you were seeing more than one guy, maybe two or three, and having sex with all of them.

Regardless of whether sex is involved or not, being cheated on can be very painful. What do most girls say they would do if they found out that a guy they were involved with had cheated on them?

# WOULD YOU BREAK UP WITH YOUR BOYFRIEND IF YOU FOUND OUT HE WAS CHEATING ON YOU?

If I found out my boyfriend was cheating on me, I would drop him so fast he wouldn't know what hit him. I don't see myself as a Mafia wife whose husband runs around with dime-store floozies.

*Marthe, 16*

I definitely don't need a two-faced two-timer. Unless I honestly believed it was a mistake and it would never happen again, I would break up with him.

*Cynthia, 17*

If he's truly sorry and begs me to take him back, and means it, I would—especially if he did it when I was away for a while and he promised never to see her again when I got back, or I had been treating him badly, or he was drunk—because I love him, and I know everyone makes mistakes.

*Lorie, 18*

If I was doing it on the side too and I didn't get caught but he did, I would give him another chance.

*Dorine, 18*

If it was the first time and he had the courage to admit it, I wouldn't break up, but I would suggest that we split up for a while and see if we miss each other.

*LaToya, 17*

If he cheated with someone I didn't know I wouldn't automatically break up—I would ask him if he still wants to be with me. But if it was with my cousin or best friend, then it would be over between us.

*Josephine, 15*

If I was walking down the street and I caught him in the act of hugging and kissing someone, I would definitely break up, but if it was hearsay, I would give him another chance.

*Liz, 16*

If he did it more than once, I would dump him because I don't believe in the sharing business, especially if I found out he had sex with the other girl—or even worse, got her pregnant.

*Beth, 17*

Sometimes a guy doesn't cheat. He goes out on a simple date, and rumors are spread and the truth gets exaggerated. I'd let it slide.

*Arielle, 16*

If I had been very faithful and honest with him, I would feel used and abused. I would keep going out with him just so I could flirt with other guys right in front of his face. I'd show him that two can play that game. What goes around comes around.

*Gwendolyn, 14*

Marthe and Cynthia are no-nonsense girls who say they would break up no matter what the situation. In reality, however, if it happened to them, chances are they'd look into the facts before making a rash decision. When you have deep feelings for someone, you don't just cut that person off without checking things out and considering the specifics of the situation. It would be like amputating a finger without finding out if it was absolutely necessary.

Wisely, most of the girls make breaking up conditioned on circumstances. Statements like "If he's sorry and promises never to do it again," "If it was the first time," "If it was the result of something I did," "If she was away," "If he was drunk," "If he didn't do it out in the open or with a close friend," "If it were a simple date and no sex was involved," and so on are an indication of their willingness to give the fellow a second chance if the circumstances aren't too incriminating.

Some girls would welcome the idea of his cheating, so that they could seize the opportunity to do the same. But why should they wait for him to take the lead, if that's how they feel?

If your boyfriend cheats on you, I suggest thinking hard about the situation. Was he deliberately trying to deceive you and make a fool of you—or did it happen for other reasons? If you were in his shoes would you think he should give you another chance or break up with you? If it were me, I'd probably give a guy at least one or two chances if he came clean with me and I was still able to have some respect for him.

I know that some people like to say that "if he cheats now, he'll cheat when he's married," and they'll tell you a relationship with such a person is doomed. But that's not necessarily true. Going out with someone is not at all the same as being married. Different standards of behavior apply. When you are married, you make a promise before God and man to be faithful to that one person. You also make a legal commitment. That's why when you want to end a marriage, you don't just walk away. You have to go to court and get it terminated before a judge. Marriage is a very serious thing—so serious that many people fear it and, out of due respect for it, refuse to make such a promise because they fear they can't keep it. They'd rather live together than get married, until they're absolutely sure they can honor the marriage vows. So, in fact, many people who cheat in relationships do so in good conscience because they know they haven't yet made that most serious commitment, the one that all the others lead up to—marriage. Your boyfriend may be perfectly capable of making such a commitment later, despite his behavior now.

## WOULD A GUY BREAK UP WITH HIS GIRLFRIEND IF HE FOUND OUT SHE WAS CHEATING?

I asked the guys the same question. Here's what they said:

It would mean I wasn't important to her, because if I was, she wouldn't risk what we had for an impulse or a momentary lapse. It may be a little self-centered, but to me it's a matter of self-respect to break up with someone who cheats on me.

*Sal, 17*

If a girl loves you, she wouldn't do anything to hurt you. The fact that she cheated means she doesn't care, so I'd break up.

*Freddy, 16*

If she's given me her word and she goes back on it, she's out. The only situation in which I wouldn't break up with her is if I had cheated on her first.

*Sam, 16*

If I really cared about her and knew she was really sorry, and she cared a lot for me, I'd give her another chance.

*Scott, 16*

If a new girlfriend was cheating on me, I would cut her off right away. But if it was someone I'd been going out with for a long time, I would give her another chance.

*Larry, 18*

I wouldn't break up with her if she could give me a good explanation as to why she did it.

*Romeo, 17*

If she cheated with a friend of mine, she'd be history, but if not, I'd take it into consideration whether or not to break up with her.

*Marty, 15*

I wouldn't break up if it was just once or twice, and she had the courage to tell me about it herself, but I would distance myself from her.

*Gabby, 17*

It depends. If she had sex with that person, I would leave her, but if she was just hugging and kissing him, I would be angry but we could talk about it. I wouldn't leave her.

*Sid, 17*

I would review the case, and if I thought I did something to provoke her actions, I would forgive her.

*Deen, 19*

I wouldn't break up, but I'd do the same to her. Maybe I'd find out that her cheating was just her way of breaking up with me.

*David, 18*

Like the girls, some guys claim they would immediately break up. Sal and Freddy, for example, are very sensitive and would take being cheated on as a rejection. But most of the guys, like most of the girls, would be willing to talk things over to see if they could continue with the relationship.

Your boyfriend may be like many of the guys just quoted—willing to look into the matter. If he really cares and you can help him to understand the circumstances, he will probably give you another chance. However, maybe you don't want another chance. As David points out, many times, when a girl cheats, it's the preliminary to breaking up—her way of saying "I'm tired of the relationship." If you are tired of it, or eager to see other guys in addition to your steady boyfriend, why not say so instead of cheating and hoping you won't get caught? Maybe you can have the best of two worlds—a steady boyfriend whom you can be honest with and the freedom to see other guys on the side.

## THE STRANGE BEHAVIOR OF JEALOUS MALES

Did your boyfriend ever act cold or mean for no apparent reason? Chances are he was stewing over the possibility of your flirting or cheating on him with other guys even if nothing could have been further from your mind. Meanwhile, since you were completely innocent, you might have interpreted his behavior to you as a bad display of temper at best, or an indication that he no longer loved you at worst.

I asked guys why they do this when they feel threatened, instead of talking to their girlfriends about the reason they were upset. If a girl had gone off to the mall with her friends, for example, and the guy was afraid that she was planning to flirt with someone else there, why didn't you just come out and say "I'm feeling jealous . . ."? I asked. Why did you hide your feelings and act mean instead? Surprisingly, every guy knew exactly what I was talking about, quickly admitted to behaving in such a way, and then told me why. Here's what they said:

We guys don't want girls to think they have power over us to get us upset so quickly.

*Dean, 18*

We're always trying not to show our real feelings. We think it's macho.

*Pierre, 16*

A guy does it because he's insecure. Boys don't want girls to think we're under their thumbs. We can't let them see we're easy to intimidate.

*Tony, 18*

I don't want her to think she can get me mad and jealous and she has me under control.

*Jay, 16*

I kept thinking about her and everyone she was with, and telling myself, no, it isn't true—and then getting mad about the whole thing.

*Leonard, 18*

I didn't want to give her the satisfaction of knowing I was jealous—and I was angry with her for being so insensitive to my feelings. The whole thing was just so embarrassing I couldn't talk about it.

*Jeff, 17*

I would have told her the truth, but I felt she might not understand and then she'd get mad at me for not trusting her, so I just stewed about it.

Tom, 17

Obviously guys feel that if they admit to being insecure about their girlfriends' feelings toward them, they will be revealing a weakness. They'd rather bury the insecurity than admit it. But the trouble is, when they do that, it comes out in other ways. The next time your boyfriend is acting strange for no apparent reason, ask yourself: "Did I just mention going somewhere without him? Could he be thinking that I was going out to flirt with other guys?" If you can bring things out in the open, maybe instead of fighting with you, he'll tell you how much you mean to him and admit at least some of his fears.

Interestingly, my sixteen-year-old daughter, Marthe, recently experienced something that I can use to demonstrate the point. A school dance was being held, and Marthe wanted to go, but her boyfriend was working that night and couldn't accompany her. She told him she was going with her friends anyway, "Just to have a good time and dance." When she said this, he replied: "I don't care. Do what you want. There are nothing but losers there anyway." Later that night when she called him, he behaved in a strange manner. He seemed distant and indifferent, and he cut the conversation short. She ended up crying after she had hung up the phone. When I asked her what was wrong, she told me that her boyfriend was being cold and cruel. "I don't think he loves me anymore," she added.

After a series of questions, I found out he had made comments about the dance like "I'll bet every Guido in the place was after you," "How many guys did you dance with?" "I can't stand those jocks that hang out at . . ." and so on. If you read between the lines, what was he really saying? "I am jealous and upset that you were away from me. I am worried that other guys were flirting with you. I'm afraid of losing you. I'm angry that I wasn't there to put a

141

stop to it." After our talk, Marthe called him back and reassured him by making comments about how much she wished he could have been at the dance with her, and how she kept thinking about him while she was there. Then she said: "You know, when you go out with your brother's band, I worry that all kinds of girls are hitting on you." He laughed, perked up, and said: "It drives me crazy to think of all those guys trying to make a move on you." They then reassured each other of their undying love. The best part about the ending is not that they lived happily ever after, but that instead of there being bad feelings based on a misunderstanding, things were brought out in the open and cleared up—even though Marthe had to use some psychology to make it happen.

## WOULD GIRLS ABOLISH CHEATING?

Girls do it. Guys do it. Yet everybody claims they don't believe in it. So what's the solution? Let's see what the girls say, and then the guys.

There's no such thing as cheating in the teen years. One guy isn't enough. It gets boring when you're only seventeen. For example, sometimes I feel like going out to the movies with another guy when my boyfriend can't go. Yet I don't want to hear about my boyfriend going to the movies with another girl, so I guess we should both just do what we have to do and be discreet about it.

*Raquel, 17*

What people call "cheating" is really part of growing up. If you don't do it now, you'll really feel cheated when you're married. Yet you can't say this to guys because they can't cope with it. I tried it once and the guy broke up with me.

*Sandra, 18*

Live and let live. He's doing the same thing and he doesn't think it's cheating.

*Nadine, 15*

As long as you're not having intimate contact, I say keep doing it. There's just too many hot guys out there to get stuck with one and play married before your time.

*Roxanne, 17*

If you tell a guy you want to see others, he'll always be suspicious of you. Therefore, you have no alternative but to "do it on the sly." People call that cheating, but I call it being smart. After all, you're only young once.

*Claudia, 15*

You should make an agreement with your boyfriend that you two are together but you can see others once in a while without telling each other. Then it wouldn't be cheating.

*Ada, 18*

Today too many teenagers act like old husbands and wives. This is our prime time, and we should live it up and have a ball. I'm not saying to jump into bed with people, just go out and find out what the world is.

*Michelle, 18*

Cheating is not damaging. It's even good because you learn whether or not you want to stay with your boyfriend. Sometimes you see you love him even more. But if you don't date others once in a while, you'll probably end up picking fights with him.

*Penny, 16*

Cheating is cheating. It's not being honest—it's deceiving. If you two agree to make a commitment, you should honor it. If you want to see others, don't have a boyfriend.

*Janice, 17*

Cheating is always wrong. Make a choice—single or committed—and stick to it.

*Joanne, 16*

Now let's see what the guys have to say. Then we'll discuss it.

143

# WOULD GUYS ABOLISH CHEATING?

If you really love someone, you have no reason to explore. If, however, you do want to see others, simply talk to your girl and explain yourself. Then you can do so with a clear conscience.

*Richie, 19*

If two people make a commitment to each other, they should not date anyone else. Yet most people do want to see others even when they're in a serious relationship. Since that's hard for either party to cope with, I say allow for human error and cheat. What's the big deal?

*Ron, 18*

We are young and want to have fun before marriage. As long as no one knows, it's okay to cheat.

*Frank, 16*

Cheating is okay as long as it's not sexual. If you're going to have sex, it should be only with your main boyfriend, and don't tell him you see others either. What he doesn't know won't hurt him.

*Judd, 17*

If you want to see others you should tell your partner. Some guys are mature enough to take it, like me for example. Then you can both openly see others.

*Milton, 18*

If you want to see others, you should have an open relationship and explain that you just can't be a one-woman man. That's all. If you insist, the girl will have to cope with it.

*Kirk, 18*

Both parties can cheat, but they don't have to tell their partners they do so. You can see people from different neighborhoods. I don't think seeing other people in the teen years is cheating. It's really just meeting new people. I'm not talking about sex of course.

*Rick, 17*

Obviously most teenagers want to see others besides their regular boyfriend or girlfriend, yet they don't want their boyfriend or girlfriend to see other people. That's where the word "cheat" comes in. It's okay for me but not for you. I want you all to myself, but you can't have me all to yourself. I only want you to think I'm faithful so you'll be faithful.

## MY SOLUTION TO THE CHEATING DILEMMA

Teenagers say "We're not married. Now's the time to explore other relationships." "Why should we be stuck with only one person?"—at the same time that they insist on fidelity from their partners. Here's what I think the solution is. If two people are going out on a steady basis, it's okay to go on a date with someone else once in a while without telling the other one, just for a change or just to check the new person out. But if you start to love that other person and want to see him a lot, then it's time to decide between the two. After all, who has time for two boyfriends anyway? It becomes a real drain of energy keeping them separate—not to mention keeping them secret.

Besides, if you try to have two regular boyfriends at the same time, you'll feel guilty because you'll be consciously deceiving at least one of them. On the other hand, if all you did was go out with someone else out of curiosity—who knows, the new one may be the love of your life, and how will you know if you don't at least check it out?—there's no reason to feel guilt. You didn't deceive anyone. You were just discreet in not making an announcement about your business until you knew whether or not it was going to lead to something. That kind of not telling isn't cheating; it's wisdom.

If you do want to go out regularly with more than one guy

or even have two or three "sort of" boyfriends at the same time, the obvious thing to do is tell the guys you're crazy about them but don't feel ready to make any commitments. Tell them you want to let things take their natural course. Then you have no obligation to tell any of the guys you're seeing details about the others. As long as they understand that you're free, they can't fault you.

## REMINDERS

1. There are different definitions of cheating—depending on who is giving the definition.
2. Most teenage girls and guys "cheat" on each other once in a while, and most don't think it's wrong under certain circumstances.
3. Some teenagers feel that there is no excuse for cheating and that if you want to see others, you should agree at the outset to an open relationship. Others feel that unless you're married, you're free to do anything you want, and you don't have to tell your partner (but that it's wise to make sure the two you're seeing live far apart).
4. Most teenagers couldn't cope with the idea of their boyfriend or girlfriend seeing others, yet they want to see others if they feel like it. In other words, they want to "cheat" but not give their partner the same privilege.
5. Most teenagers would listen to reason if they found out their boyfriend or girlfriend were cheating.
6. If your boyfriend suddenly starts behaving in an indifferent way for no apparent reason, chances are, his attitude could be a camouflage for feelings of jealousy—especially if you've recently been in situations where he thinks you might have met other guys. If this is so, bring things out in the open in a subtle way and try to calm his fears.
7. In my opinion, it's okay not to tell your partner when you go out with someone else every once in a while. However, if you begin seeing that other person often, or

start having deep feelings for him, it's time to decide between the two—otherwise you'll feel as if you are deceiving at least one of them, and you'll feel guilty. Alternately, you could be open about the fact that you don't feel ready to make a commitment and date as many guys as you want to.

# 9

# When He's Not
# Worth Keeping

It's great to have a boyfriend, especially in the beginning when things are going well, but it's not so much fun when, after a while, you find yourself in a state of constant turmoil. You may begin to wonder if it's worth the grief.

In this chapter we'll discuss a variety of situations in which a relationship has become more trouble than it's worth. We'll talk about the "bossman," the "perpetual liar," the "druggie," the guy who never has time for you, the man who's engaged in illegal activities, the fellow who likes to keep his women in line with a whack or two, the guy who is "out for one thing only," the gent who causes you to lose sight of your goal, the cad who constantly puts you down, and the guy who is always arguing with you. And last but not least, we'll discuss the boy who leaves you for someone else and talk about why he too is not really worth keeping. Then we'll end up with advice from other teenagers on what to watch out for so that you don't get involved with the wrong guy in the first place.

## THE BOSS MAN AND THE
## JEALOUS BOYFRIEND

In the beginning it's flattering when a guy takes such a great interest in you that he wants to get involved in all the details of your life. After all, he loves you and he's concerned about you—or so he tells you. When he asks you not to wear certain outfits because they are too "sexy," you're flattered because you think "He's afraid other guys will look at me. He wants me all to himself." When he wants you to account for every minute spent away from him, you're happy to do so because you like the experience of being adored. But trouble is just around the corner when these kinds of behavior surface.

My boyfriend started out normal with me. But little by little he began taking over my life—like a father. He told me what to wear, chose my friends for me, and even scolded me for wearing too much makeup. He said it was to attract guys. When I went to co-ed dance class he said, "I don't want you wearing those leotards. I know how guys think." He would watch me with stern eyes when I joked around with people. I was always looking over my shoulder for him, worried about what he would say. I broke it off because he was too possessive.

*Carol, 17*

If you find that you can't be yourself anymore when your boyfriend is around, it's time to get away from him. If a guy makes you feel as if you have to check yourself every time you open your mouth or put on an outfit, you're being stifled and the sooner you cut yourself loose from him, the better. You don't need him. There are other guys out there who will enjoy you for your own unique style, and who will celebrate rather than squash your personality.

We all understand that if a guy cares about his girl, he's going to be somewhat jealous when other guys pay attention to her, but some guys go overboard.

149

I really loved my boyfriend, Tommy, but I had to break up with him because I just couldn't take it anymore. Any time I would talk to a guy, even a guy who was just a friend, he would immediately accuse me of doing things with him. After five months of torture, one day Tommy's friend who is like a brother to me gave me a hug and a friendly kiss, and Tommy was right there to see it. The next day Tommy said, "I saw you kiss my friend. What do you think you're playing me for? A fool?" He called me names and everything. I thought about what my mother said, that very jealous guys are insecure and there's no satisfying them. I told him I wanted to call it quits, and he left angry. After that he tried to make up but I wouldn't go back because I kept remembering how miserable he made my life.

*Lisa, 16*

Imagine going with a guy like Tommy. You can forget about peace of mind. You'd spend most of your time worrying that he might misinterpret any innocent thing you did. Unless they get help, teenage Tommys grow into adult Tommys, and they're a guarantee of a life of misery. In fact, I had an ex-boyfriend who reminds me of Tommy. One night we went out to a piano bar, and after a while Joe excused himself and went to the men's room. The moment he left, a good-looking man started up a conversation with me. Knowing how jealous Joe was, I immediately said, "I can't talk to you. I'm with someone." (I felt like a fool saying this because the man had merely commented on the great music, but I knew that Joe would make a scene if he came back and saw us talking.) The man looked at me as if I were crazy and said, "I didn't ask you to marry me. I just wanted to have a conversation." I laughed and we continued to talk.

A few minutes later Joe came back, and sure enough, he was furious. He walked straight up to the man and said: "You want her phone number? I'll give it to you. She's all yours. You can take her home if you want to." I got up and walked out of the club. Needless to say, we had a big fight that night, and we broke up shortly thereafter. I was madly in love with the guy, but the relationship just wasn't worth the constant worry and tension. With him I had to be vigilant at all times, on guard, and I always had to explain myself—even though I had done nothing wrong.

If your boyfriend's jealousy is so out of hand that he keeps you continually on edge, it's time to walk, and fast.

## THE PERPETUAL LIAR

Most people (and probably even George Washington himself) have told a lie or two in their lives. But what do you do when you find that your boyfriend has trouble distinguishing the truth from fiction?

I went out with this guy and he told me he had a Ferrari, but it was at his uncle's house in storage for the winter. He also claimed he was going to inherit a fortune from his rich uncle and that his father was the president of a company. After we were going out for about three weeks, I started catching him in little lies. Later I found out his father was a sanitation worker. Everything he had told me about himself was a lie. He even lied about where he worked. He said he was the manager at a bank when he really worked in Burger King. I confronted him and told him he didn't have to lie to me, because I liked him for himself, but he got mad and made up other lies to cover his original lies. Finally I realized he was sick and needed mental help, and we broke up.

*Sue, 15*

Sue is right. The boy needs help. Apparently his self-esteem is so low that he believes he must make up lies about himself in order to be worthy of acceptance. If I were Sue, I would gently suggest that he get professional help, emphasizing that he would feel a great relief once he didn't have the need to ''cover up'' his real self.

If you've ever been involved with a perpetual liar, you know that the relationship is doomed, because there's really no way to get close to someone who hides behind a mask of fantasy. Such a relationship is endless frustration. Who needs it?

Many perpetual liars are as victimized by their own lies as the people they lie to. They're trapped by their own desperation. But they just lie for their own convenience, in order to control people. They're not pathological—they're simply dishonest.

One minute he's lying about where he's going, the next minute he's lying about where he's been. Then he lies about when he's going to call, and when he doesn't, he lies about why he didn't call. Next he lies about other girls he's seeing, and when you find out for sure, he lies about not seeing them again—but of course he does, and when you catch him, he lies about what happened. With a guy like this you know you can't win because he's always going to have a story to tell. Take it from me. I spent seven months going out with a guy like this.

*Rosy, 18*

Guys who engage in this kind of dishonesty are enough to make you want to pull your hair out, bang your head against the wall, break up your room, scream at the top of your lungs, cry yourself into hysteria, or even question your own sanity.

If you've met one of these fellows, you know it. I'm not talking about the poor soul who gets caught lying once or twice because he was hoping you wouldn't find out about the date he had or the girl he flirted with in study hall. I'm discussing the guy who lies *all the time*, for convenience sake, as a way of manipulating you. This is the kind of guy who makes up lies so that he can keep things going his way. His whole life is a cheat. He thinks any lie is acceptable, so long as he can get away with it. He's often a professional charmer as well as a perpetual liar—the two things seem to go together—and he's dangerous because he can wreak havoc on your emotions. You love him, so you want to believe him, but all the time you know you're a fool to trust him. Each time you give him another chance, you hate yourself, because you know you're a fool for doing so. If you stay in such a relationship, you'll eventually despise yourself for putting up with it.

No guy is worth the loss of your self-esteem. Even if it's painful, it's better to break up with a guy than destroy your image of yourself. You won't be sorry once time has passed and the pain has faded. In fact, you'll be enormously relieved to have him out of your life and proud of yourself for having had the courage to get rid of him. Guys like this are nothing but trouble—and they don't change. Or at any rate, they very rarely do. So don't fool yourself into thinking you'll be the one to change him. That's one reason why they don't change—because there's always someone willing to give them another chance.

## THE DRUGGIE

Not everyone who does drugs looks like an addict. There are some well-groomed, handsome, intelligent guys who indulge. These are the ones you have to watch out for, because they can take you by surprise. A guy who does coke to help him lift his spirits, or who smokes pot to relax is drug-dependent, no matter what he tells you about how he's got his habit under control. If you become involved with someone like that, he can prove to be more than just a bad influence on you—he can be your undoing.

I met this guy, Adam, and he seemed really cool. He was a great dresser and really funny and intelligent. Eventually we started going out. But every time we were together, he would do coke. He would always offer me some, and I felt so stupid always saying no. One time I did the coke and I couldn't get to sleep all night. The next day I felt scared. I imagined my brain like in the TV ad, where you see a frying pan with hot oil and they break an egg into the pan, and say: "This is your brain. This is your brain on drugs." And you see your brain frying. It got to the point where I couldn't go out with him any more, because I knew I would end up doing more and more coke. After we broke up, I found out he was in a rehab center.

*Pat, 16*

If you're going with a guy you know will be a bad influence on you, no matter how much you like him, he's not worth it. You have to think of your own survival. Remember this: No matter how much in love you are now, if you allow yourself to go down the wrong path, once you're there, you'll be there alone, and the one who led you there will be long gone—or helpless himself. When your grades go down, when you don't make the college of your choice, when you end up without a good job and maybe on public assistance, or worse, collecting empty soda cans or even homeless, you'll wonder then when the big party stopped and where all the merrymakers have gone.

Of course the worst way to end up is dead. It so happens that a very high percentage of people who die before their time die drug-related deaths. I recently read a best-selling book by Malcolm Forbes entitled *They Went That a Way*, which tells how famous people died. In reading the stories Forbes tells, I discovered what the majority of people who died at an early age did so because of drugs—even in the 1940s and '50s. Although street drugs weren't as popular or available then as they are now, many actors, artists, and musicians did have access to drugs, which may explain why so many of them died so young. So if anyone tells you "drugs don't do any harm if you don't overdo it," don't believe him. It's the biggest lie ever told.

Don't fool yourself into thinking that coke and crack are the only dangerous drugs either. There's a more subtle, mellow kind of drug, which can also cause a lot of problems. A little weed here, a little weed there, and before you know it, you've destroyed your motivation.

None of my friends do drugs—not even marijuana. But this guy I was going out with would light up a joint every time we went out, and he would ask me if I wanted to try it to mellow me out. I did try it a few times and it made me sleepy, and then hungry, but it didn't really do that much for me. He said sometimes it takes awhile to get used to it. I thought about it and said to myself, "Why should I want to work on this when so many people are trying to get off drugs?" Then I thought about how he's not doing too well in school and doesn't really have a goal or anything. After that it started to annoy me when he smoked because I noticed he would act stupid. It was like we were in a different head or something.

*Rochelle, 17*

When I think about marijuana, another TV commercial comes to mind—the one where a guy in his early thirties is in his room smoking a joint with his friend and he says: "Man, nothing happens if you smoke marijuana." Then his mother yells up the stairs, "Joe, did you look for a job today?" The guy opens the window and starts fanning the smoke and he yells down, "Yeah, Ma. I'll look tomorrow." The the narrator comes in and says: "Right. Nothing happens if you smoke marijuana."

Years ago, in the sixties, when everyone thought it was cool to smoke marijuana, and before they had proof that it destroys motivation and the ability to think and solve mathematical problems, I sensed that it was harmful, because I noticed that friends who smoked it were lazy. They lacked drive and energy, and didn't seem to care about their goals.

Yes indeed. Marijuana mellows you out. It makes you so mellow you really don't want to push yourself at all. If there's anything we need, it's more drive, not less. So smoking weed is like working against yourself. Not very bright, is it?

155

# WHEN YOUR BOYFRIEND NEGLECTS YOU

We've already discussed how important it is for a guy to spend time with other guys, and how people in relationships need to give each other space in order to keep the fire burning. Neglect is something entirely different. When a guy is never around, when he's always making excuses not to see you, something is wrong.

My boyfriend doesn't call me for a week at a time, and when I call him, he makes up some excuse, like he has to work or he is busy. He only sees me when he has nothing better to do. He acts like it's all about him, and I don't even count—and I should be lucky that he sees me at all. Obviously, I care about him much more than he cares about me.

*Jackie, 14*

Jackie's right. The only thing she can do is break up with the guy before he breaks up with her. Sometimes that brings a guy to his senses, but don't count on it. Most times the kind of neglect Jackie describes means he doesn't care, and there's nothing to be done to revive his fading feelings for you. If you find yourself in the position of having to beg your boyfriend to spend time with you, it's time to acknowledge that he's not as committed to the relationship as you are. It's much better to find a guy who is at least as eager to see you as you are to see him; otherwise you'll feel like a beggar.

Sometimes your boyfriend neglects you not because he doesn't care about you, but because it's extremely difficult for him to get to see you. He may care about you a lot, but that won't help either of you if you never get to be together.

I dropped one of my boyfriends because he lived in Manhattan and I lived in Brooklyn, and he never came to see me. When I asked him why he never came to see me he would say he had too much homework or he couldn't get home late for dinner. He expected me to go out there, but my mother didn't want me making such a long trip either.

*Marissa, 16*

I met this guy on vacation, and we spent the whole summer as boyfriend and girlfriend. When we got home, he lived about an hour away from me by car and even though he had a car, after a while, he stopped coming as often as he used to. It was depressing because I loved him so much.

*Tama, 17*

"Geographically undesirable" is the phrase I use to describe a situation where two people live too far apart to get together often. As unromantic as it sounds, if the love of your life lives far away, the relationship has a very slim chance of surviving. You may say to yourself "If he really loved me, he would go to the ends of the earth to be with me." Well, if it's meant to be, maybe he will, or perhaps you two will meet again some day, farther up the road. Otherwise accept the facts. He's geographically undesirable.

## THE DRUG DEALER AND THE THIEF

Did you ever go out with a guy who was "loaded," even though you knew that he'd gotten his money in a dishonest way? In other words, his money was "dirty." It may even have been blood money, gotten at the expense of someone else's life.

If you go out with a guy like this, it won't be long before you lose respect not just for him, but for yourself as well, because his actions fly in the face of common decency.

My boyfriend always wore lots of gold, and he would buy me very expensive presents and give me money too. I knew he was dealing drugs, but I kept pushing it out of my mind because he wasn't doing drugs, just dealing them. When we'd talk about it, he would tell me that it didn't matter because the people he sold to would be buying it from someone else if not from him—but still it ate away at me. I didn't respect him because I thought, "Great goal in life. To sell drugs and make quick money," and here I was trying to get high marks so I could get into a good college and eventually go to law school. The more I thought about it, the more ashamed I was to be going out with a guy who had no values. He turned me off, so eventually I ended it.

*Rita, 16*

As discussed before, it *is* a turn-off to realize that your boyfriend's values are in total opposition to yours. Anyone who reasons that it's okay to sell drugs because people will only buy them from someone else anyway is lacking in the morality department. His attitude is: "As long as I get mine, it doesn't matter what happens to anyone else." He thinks nothing of taking an illegal shortcut in order to beat the system that would otherwise require him to work hard. In fact, it's guys like that whom Rita might end up sending to jail after she graduates from law school. Imagine how you would feel about such a guy if you'd always been taught to respect hard work—not to mention the law.

What about the thief?

I was in love with this guy. He was gorgeous—tall, with jet-black hair and light-blue eyes, and what a body! But he got his money from stealing cars. I knew because he would go out of state with a friend and come back with a strange car, then take it apart and sell the parts. When I asked where he got the cars, he would tell me he found them and laugh. Finally he got caught and went to jail. Great boyfriend. I'm just glad I wasn't with him when the cops stopped him.

*Tara, 16*

Dirty money is just that. It's dirty, and it makes you feel sullied to have it spent on you. It's as if the dirt rubs off on you, even though you didn't steal the money yourself. I'm not just talking abstract morality either. If Tara or Rita were ever on the scene when the cops came after their boyfriends, they might end up in trouble too, no matter how innocent they were.

## THE VIOLENT GUY

Why would a girl stay with a guy even after he has slapped her face or pushed her around? Often she is unwilling to face the fact that his behavior is part of a recurrent pattern. She keeps hoping each episode will be the last one.

Every time my boyfriend got upset, he would hit me and call me dirty names. Then he would make up and say he was sorry, and act so sweet, that I would have to forgive him. After a while he would do it again—give me a black eye, etc., and each time I would swear that I wasn't going to take it any more. One day he really hurt me and I had to go to the hospital. I was so angry that I told them the truth. They convinced me to press charges and I did.

*Joanne, 18*

Chances are, if your boyfriend has ever hit you you think this section does not apply to you. But it must apply to someone, because there are millions of cases of wife and girlfriend abuse across the country every year.

This kind of abuse doesn't start in the adult years. It is usually learned in the early childhood years, as children see their parents being violent to each other. The only cure for it is professional help. If your boyfriend hits you, don't think of it as an isolated incident. You can be sure it will happen again, so the best thing to do is think of your own well-being and get out before you become any more involved. The longer you wait, the greater the emotional wrench when you finally decide to leave.

If, however, you find yourself willing to tolerate abuse from a guy, *you* have a problem. It's the battered woman syndrome—which encompasses everything from a slap to an actual beating. Women who allow themselves to be battered are in desperate need of therapy. If you see this tendency in yourself, and you don't feel that you can talk to your parents about getting help, speak to your school guidance counselor who can put you in touch with free counseling. If you're over eighteen, you have access to 800 numbers in every state that offer help to women who are physically abused. Call information and the operator will give you the number. Many of these are run by state agencies that can offer counseling in addition to physical protection. Fortunately for you, you're at an age when help can work fast and effectively, because you're young enough that patterns of abuse haven't yet had time to become established. But it's your decision to become mentally healthy. No one can make it for you.

## THE GUY WHO CAUSES YOU TO LOSE SIGHT OF YOUR GOALS

I was recently discussing the book *The Assistant*, by Bernard Malamud, with my high-school students. In the book Morris, now miserable with his life, complains that he never became a pharmacist because his wife-to-be insisted that he buy a grocery store instead, believing that it would earn more money. I asked my students: "Whose fault is it that Morris didn't become a pharmacist?" All but one said: "It was his wife's fault." But the holdout was the only one who was correct. No one was to blame but Morris himself. He let his wife persuade him to take the wrong path. He took the shortcut to what he believed would be "easy money" out of weakness. Evidently he didn't really want to pay the price of the long, hard years of schooling. Now, again out of weakness, rather than taking the blame for his own shortcomings in the past, he blames his wife. But all the blaming in the world will not erase the facts. We are each responsible for our own destiny, and if we miss it, the fault lies within ourselves.

Very often women give up their career goals to please a man or to follow him where his career leads him. This is a big mistake. Fortunately, these days, it doesn't happen as often as it used to. Yet even today many young women go to college and, the minute they meet an aspiring doctor or lawyer, abandon their own goals in life to put their man through school, and then get permanently sidetracked because they are "barefoot and pregnant," as the saying goes.

Did they make a worthy sacrifice, or did they seize upon a convenient opportunity to avoid the challenges of working to achieve professional success? It's hard to judge another person's decisions—what's right for you may make me miserable. If this decision makes them happy, that's fine. Usually it doesn't, however, and then what you hear is that their husbands "made" them give up their careers. In reality, however, who is to blame? Surely not the man. Often the pattern for this kind of behavior is set in high school, when these girls began throwing aside their friends, their hobbies, and their goals for the current boy in their lives. Hello! Does this describe anyone you know?

When I was going into my senior year in high school, I was planning to become a policewoman. When our class visited the police academy, I met a cop and started going out and we fell in love. Once I graduated school, he told me that he didn't want me to be a cop because it was too dangerous, so I became a secretary. Now I hate my job, but he says if I want to stay with him, he won't let me be a cop. I don't know what to do because I love him.

*Pamela, 19*

When I hear the word "let," alarm bells go off in my head. That word should never enter into a male-female relationship. Words such as "wish" and "want," "hope"

161

and "like" are okay. But "let" always means trouble. You are not a child and your boyfriend is not your father. You're an adult, and you must decide for yourself what is and is not right for you. If you forfeit to a man the right to make decisions about your goals, you do yourself a tremendous disservice. You may end up spending a lot of your adulthood crying about "the road not taken." It's so much more fun to find out what you "could have done" by doing it in the first place. After all, you're not asking the guy in your life to give up his goals for you, so why should he deny you the chance to achieve yours? It's just not fair, and I hope you won't let him get away with it. If you do, you'll have only yourself to blame.

## THE GUY WHO HITS ON YOU

By now you know that teenage guys are very eager to get their hands on you, and you realize it's a perfectly natural instinct because they're at their sexual peak. However, just because they want something doesn't mean you have to give it to them. Nobody ever died of horniness.

Guys who refuse to respect a girls' wishes are those who are obviously not interested in the girl as a person, but rather as a means to an end—a vehicle to satisfy sexual urges. Recently I received this letter from a reader.

Dear Dr. Vedral:
I think we need a book about fast-working guys. What do you do if he tries to get up your shirt and down your pants? If you don't let him, he'll go to school and make everybody believe you're really a nerd and not "cool." I'm not afraid to admit I'm still a virgin. Now he wants to do EVERYTHING. What should I do?

*Gina, 14*

If this happens to you, first of all, you remove his hand from your shirt area with your right hand and his other hand from your pants area with your left hand. You then look him straight in the eye and say "Read my lips. *NO.*" If that doesn't stop him, the next time you remove his hands, you slap them as if to say "You naughty boy." Then repeat: "I said no." If he still doesn't get the message, you tell him that if he can't respect your wishes, he obviously doesn't care about you. Then tell him good luck and good-bye.

If he tells people at school you're a nerd, they'll think the opposite. They'll respect you for not being "easy." In fact, he would be doing you a favor if he spread such rumors about you. Guys treasure girls with such a reputation.

What should you do if the only time a guy wants to be with you is when the two of you can be alone?

I used to go with this guy and every time we would see each other, we would go to his house and he would try to have sex with me. When I said I didn't want to, he said I didn't love him and I didn't care about his needs. Later I found out he used to do the same thing to this other girl in my class, and he even used the same line. That's when I realized he was out for one thing only and I broke up with him.

*Cynthia, 16*

If your guy only wants to see you when the two of you can be alone, at which time he always makes an "approach," it's obvious what he wants, and it isn't an intellectual conversation. If a guy really likes a girl for herself, for her personality and her inner being as well as for her looks and her sexuality, he'll be willing to take no for an answer. He may want to have sex with her, but he'll certainly respect her right to say no, and most assuredly he won't force himself on her or become angry because she refuses his wishes. It may hurt to leave your boyfriend once you discover the truth about his intentions, but it will hurt a lot less than feeling used if you stay with him and let him take advantage of you.

# THE GUY WHO CONSTANTLY
## PUTS YOU DOWN

What kind of a guy would continually insult you—call you fat, make fun of your hair, imply that you're stupid, laugh at you when you make a mistake, and generally focus on your faults? An insecure guy, that's who.

My boyfriend always insults me—to the point where I want to cry. I can't do anything right around him. If I'm trying to play tennis, when I miss the ball, he calls me a ditz and laughs at me. When I was learning to drive, he mocked me because I had trouble parking, and when he found out I scored lower than he did on the SATs, he said I was a dumb blonde. I really love him, but I wonder why he's always insulting me. If I'm that bad, why is he going out with me?

*Laura, 18*

He's going out with her because she's a willing whipping post. Guys who put others down do so because they have such low self-esteem that they need to bring others down in order to feel okay about themselves. However, it never works. The more they put people down, the lower they sink in their own eyes.

You *could* take on the job of trying to help this guy feel better about himself. However, you would have to talk constantly about all the positive qualities you see in him and compliment him incessantly on his achievements, no matter how minor. It's a big job, and more than likely, you won't be able to do it alone. His parents and a therapist will be needed, too. Do you want to spend your teenage years dealing with someone else's ego problems? Aren't your own enough to deal with? You certainly won't be getting any help from this guy.

# THE BICKERING BOYFRIEND

What about the guy who keeps you in a state of turmoil because the two of you are arguing all the time? If this is you and your boyfriend, you're probably incompatible.

I was going out with this guy who disagreed with everything I did and said—and I disagreed with a lot of his ideas, too. For example, he played in a rock band, and I thought that was a stupid waste of time. I played violin and he mocked me because it was classical music. He would wear punk-rocker clothing and I thought he looked dirty. I'm more the preppy type. He couldn't stand my way of talking and I couldn't stand his. He made fun of my "uptight" corporate father, and I would talk about his truckdriver father. I love the ballet and he hated it. He loves football and I hate it. If we saw a movie together, I would think the ending meant one thing, and he would say it meant another. We would even argue over which is the best car or who is the strongest fighter. After a while I think I hated him. You may wonder why we went out in the first place. Well, he was sooo gorgeous and all the girls in the school were in love with him, and I'm a cheerleader, so I guess that turned him on.

*Tracy, 17*

Here's a classic example of two people who get together for superficial reasons—initial physical attraction and the desire to make an impression on others. Then they wonder why it isn't working out. As discussed before, it takes more than looks or sexual attraction or even popularity to make a relationship work.

If you find yourself constantly riled up when you're with your boyfriend, maybe it's time you asked yourself what you two have in common. If it's just physical attraction or a need for social status, you might want to reevaluate whether you belong together.

# WHAT CAN YOU DO IF YOUR BOYFRIEND LEAVES YOU FOR SOMEONE ELSE?

The last case, and the real heartbreaker, is when you're still in love with a guy and he leaves you for someone else. You find it hard to accept and you wish he were still yours. But no matter how much in love with him you are, *he's not worth keeping* anyway, because if he doesn't love you, you're dancing without a partner, and that's definitely no fun.

Many girls have had this happen to them. Here's their advice on how to react when it happens to you:

It was probably for the best. He could have been cheating on you when he was going out with you.

*Anne, 17*

Don't be sad. Make yourself more beautiful than before and get yourself a better boyfriend. Then he'll feel stupid.

*Maria, 18*

If he left you, he's a fool, and who wants to go out with a fool anyway.

*Joyce, 16*

Don't run after him. It's a waste of time. You're young and there are more fish in the sea just waiting to be caught.

*Melissa, 17*

Don't just sit around singing the blues. Get yourself back on track. Go out and meet new people.

*Leona, 14*

First of all, don't ever give a boy all of you. In case he dumps you, you have something to fall back on.

*Sharon, 16*

Don't get mad, get even. Go out with one of his friends.

*Trina, 17*

Buck up. He probably wasn't worth it anyway. Always have someone on the side, just in case.

*Judy, 13*

When my boyfriend left me for another girl, I felt ugly, but then I thought, someday someone will leave him and he'll feel that way, too.

*Nadine, 15*

Don't let it get to you or take it as rejection. It doesn't mean there's something wrong with you at all or that the other girl is better than you. You just weren't right for him.

*Marthe, 16*

The advice is clear. Look at the positive side. It was probably for the best. Go out there and meet new people. It's natural to wonder if something is wrong with you if your boyfriend drops you for someone else, but if you think about it, you'll realize that your boyfriend left you not because of some lack in you, but because of a whole set of needs of his own—needs that have nothing to do with you. As mentioned before, teenagers are still in the process of finding out who is compatible with them, and they will and should go through many relationships before they settle into a permanent one, namely marriage.

Everyone goes through a breakup, and most people are likely to feel rejected if they didn't do the breaking up. The thing to do is to realize that you've also broken up with guys in your lifetime, and these guys will find other girls who think they're terrific, just as you'll find other guys who think you're terrific. Personally, I think it's too cynical to keep "someone on the side, just in case." You won't feel the need to do this if you have enough self-confidence to know that when one relationship ends, you'll start another soon enough.

## GIRLS TELL WHOM TO WATCH OUT FOR

What are the warning signs for guys you should avoid? How do you know when you should run the opposite way? I

167

asked girls to tell us from their own experience who the real problem guys are. They say:

The ones who are touchy-feely all the time. They have their minds on one track and try to force you into doing something you don't want to do by saying "If you loved me ..."

*Tami, 18*

Guys who proclaim their love on the first three days of dating you, or make moves in the first stages of hanging out.

*Marthe, 16*

Guys who get you drunk at a party and say everything you want to hear, just for their own satisfaction.

*Kim, 16*

Guys who want you to go to bed the first time you meet. They're not coming back, if you know what I mean.

*Sonia, 17*

Guys who never want to go out, just stay home and "fool around." They rarely call you and when they do it's to try to use you for money.

*Jessica, 15*

Guys who are "studs" and have lots of friends who are all girls. They think they're Casanovas.

*Rio, 17*

Guys who are disrespectful, rough, and impolite. Also those who are lazy and don't like to work.

*Linda, 14*

## GUYS TELL WHOM TO WATCH OUT FOR

If you listened carefully to what the girls said, I think you should pay even stricter attention to what the guys say, because some of them are talking about themselves. Take it from the guys. Watch out for:

Sugar-tongued fast talkers who are always saying things like "I love you, you are everything I ever wanted, I will be with you forever . . ." at the same time that they are trying to get you into their bedrooms. All they really want is you-know-what.

*Jake, 18*

Guys who try to flatter you with expensive gifts and have big bankrolls, because when they get what they want, they are gone.

*Randall, 19*

Guys who tell you they love you and try to get romantic real quick.

*Tyrone, 18*

Guys who put on an act to look cool. That's a sign of insecurity.

*Steven, 16*

Guys who think of themselves all the time and think they're God's gift to women. They're the ones who will use and abuse you.

*Orlando, 17*

Girls, most guys are only after one thing. Don't give it to them.

*Michael, 16*

Guys who are loud and boisterous and are always cutting school, who don't want to meet your family and who have a bad reputation.

*Wally, 15*

It's a strange thing about human nature. Sometimes we know that something is wrong, and yet we plunge right ahead and do it anyway, only to get hurt. But we don't have to continue making the same mistake. We can learn from our own and other people's experience. A word to the wise is sufficient.

169

## REMINDERS

1. The following fellows are not worth keeping:

   - Bossy, jealous, controlling guys.
   - Guys who lie all the time.
   - Guys who do drugs.
   - Guys who are always too busy to see you or who are "geographically undesirable."
   - Guys who are engaged in illegal activities.
   - Guys who raise a hand to you—no matter what the reason. There's *no* good reason.
   - Guys who try to make you lose sight of your goals.
   - Guys who are "out for one thing only."
   - Guys who are constantly putting you down.
   - Guys who are continually arguing with you.

2. If your boyfriend broke up with you, realize that no matter how much you love him, or how much it hurts, he's not worth keeping, because if he doesn't love you, you're dancing without a partner, and that's no fun.

3. The higher your self-esteem, the more likely you are to form positive, nourishing relationships, so continue to pursue your goals and work on knowing and loving who you are. That's the person who will someday attract a man who values you and is worthy of you.

# 10

# Living Without a Boyfriend and Loving It

I'm better off having a boyfriend because I am the type of person who cannot be alone. When I am alone, I feel terrified, unwanted, and worthless.

*Alice, 15*

Alice wrote these words in answer to the question "Can you be happy without a boyfriend?" Sad, isn't it. Well, even if you don't feel as destitute as Alice when you don't have a boyfriend, if you do feel alone, left out, or even slightly unhappy, this chapter is for you.

Boyfriends are great to have, and as you might have gathered by now, I'm certainly not against them. Otherwise, why would I have devoted the first three chapters to telling you how to get one? What I am opposed to, however, is your feeling that without a boyfriend, your life is meaningless and you are worthless. Simply put, I'm opposed to the idea that any girl allows a guy to become her major reason for living. This kind of thinking will always get a girl in trouble. Why?

If you center your entire life around a guy, what will happen if he breaks up with you? You'll feel as if you can't go on without him. But worse than that, if you get into the habit of centering your life around your boyfriend now, you'll do the same thing in the future and eventually marry someone through whom you expect to live. This is bound to result in unhappiness. Let me explain.

When you meet someone and fall in love, it's important to keep your "self" separate from that person, no matter how much you love him. In other words, it's not a good idea to surrender your personality to him or try to live your life through him. Otherwise, if he should leave you—and given the high breakup rate of teenage romance, that's not unlikely—you'll feel like Alice: terrified, unwanted, and worthless. It's as if there's no "you" there once he's gone, because you've so entirely based your identity on being with him.

It reminds me of the television show *War of the Worlds*, where creatures take over people's bodies and then begin to run their lives. On the show, when the creatures attack, the shocked person is unable to defend himself as the invader seeps through his skin until it has fillled up his entire being with its monstrous essence. In a matter of minutes the engulfed person is "one of them." The person continues to look like himself, but in reality only his appearance is his own. His actions are now those of the invader. Sound like anyone you know?

Unlike the people in the science fiction–based television show, you have the power to defend yourself from such an invasion. You don't have to merge your personality with your boyfriend's. You don't have to abandon your goals, your hobbies, and your friends and devote your full energy to him. No one can live through another person. We must each find out what our "job" in life is, and do it.

Your "job" in life will become apparent when you begin to develop those natural talents that constitute your potential. The more you do this, the closer you come to being a complete person or, to put it another way, to becoming what psychologists call "self-actualized." The happiest people, the most successful people, the people with the greatest peace of mind and inner joy, and those who contribute the most to the world are those who are highly self-actualized.

On the other hand, those people who do not find out what their talent is and develop it, those people who do not move in the direction of self-actualization are the ones most likely to be heard complaining that life has given them a bad deal, or making jealous comments regarding other people's successes. Often they have denied themselves their own opportunities for achievement and success by trying to live their lives through someone else—an attempt doomed to failure, because in the long run it is impossible to find self-fulfillment through reflected glory.

While building your life around your boyfriend is bad practice for the future, having a boyfriend and learning how to fit him into your life in a healthy way is good practice. The goal of this chapter, then, is not to discourage you from having boyfriends, but to show you how to keep their role in your life in perspective, so that they can become an asset rather than a liability.

We'll talk about how to be happy when all of your friends have a boyfriend except you. We'll discuss your goals and how boyfriends can affect them, and we'll talk about how to cope with breaking up with a guy you've been going out with for a long time. We'll end up with a discussion on how to be happy with or without a boyfriend.

## THERE *ARE* ADVANTAGES TO HAVING A BOYFRIEND

It feels great to have a boyfriend. You have someone to go out with—guaranteed dates with a guy you love. You have someone to be affectionate with, a person you can hug and kiss and cuddle with. You have a friend of the opposite sex who will comfort you and take your side when life isn't going your way. You have a ready pal to go places with and to have fun with, and someone to spend time with when you're bored. In addition, you have someone to parade around with in front of your friends, someone whose specialness makes you feel special. Last but not least, you have protection against feeling left out, especially if all of your friends have boyfriends.

## WHEN ALL OF YOUR FRIENDS HAVE A BOYFRIEND AND YOU DON'T

Sometimes even the most popular of girls end up boyfriend-less at a time when it seems that every other girl in the world has a boyfriend. How does it feel when you're the only one in your crowd without a steady? Girls who answered this question were frank about the pain they felt.

I thought of myself as a loser, not as good as them, not as pretty.

*Lisa, 17*

I felt ugly and skinny and not worth having, and I got an inferiority complex.

*Keisha, 15*

I felt it was my job to prove I could have a boyfriend if I wanted one.

*Betsy, 16*

I felt like grabbing the first bum in the street.

*Jennifer, 14*

I felt kind of lonely, because I didn't have anyone to talk to or hang around with. And I felt like a third wheel when I hung out with my friends and their boyfriends.

*Marnie, 16*

I hated when they would talk about what they were doing on Friday night, and I had to be all quiet.

*Mary, 16*

Feeling left out is no fun. How can you help but feel this way, especially if your friends, who used to spend their time with you, now spend most of their time with their boyfriends?

174

But what's even worse than feeling left out is the fear that something is wrong with you, and that that's why you don't have a boyfriend. You begin to magnify your faults. You probably begin with your physical appearance, blaming your dateless state on your braces, your acne, your weight, your red hair, your crooked nose, your brown eyes, your big thighs, and so on. But then you may look around you and notice that girls much less attractive than you have boyfriends. So obviously your looks are not really the problem. A lot of help that thought is!

"If it's not looks, then there must be something else wrong with me," you say to yourself. Then you start to wonder if the guys have looked beneath the surface and seen that you're a bad person and are therefore unlovable. You wonder if they know something about you that you don't know. Perhaps you were born with some mysterious fault. You begin to doubt your worth as a person.

Don't worry. Almost everyone feels this way from time to time. The feeling usually stems from insecurity that begins as early as infancy. When a baby is not loved the way he or she needs to be loved, that baby comes to believe that the fault lies within. "If I'm not loved, I must not be lovable," the baby concludes. Of course, I don't mean to suggest that your parents did not love you, or to blame them. It's just that no parent is capable of perfect love, and all of us are the products of our parents' imperfect love, just as they themselves are the products of *their* parents' imperfect love. The insecurity that results causes some people to spend years in therapy, just trying to realize that they are indeed lovable.

Whenever you start experiencing those "unlovable feelings," why not try this? Picture yourself as an infant in the cradle. See your sweet, innocent, baby face, eagerly waiting for Mommy to come and pick you up. But then watch what happens when Mommy doesn't pick you up—perhaps because she's making dinner and trying to keep an eye on your older brother who's just beginning to walk (you fill in the correct details of *your* family life), perhaps because she had a terrible day at work and has fallen asleep exhausted.

175

Of course, you do not know this and are not capable of understanding anyway, so you feel abandoned and scared and begin to howl. Then in your mind, go to yourself and pick yourself up and say, "I love you. You *are* lovable. Nothing is wrong with you. You're an adorable, innocent baby." Then pick the baby up and hug her until you feel her being reassured and satisfied. Do this every time you feel unlovable. It's such a simple yet healing thing to do. In time, those feelings of being unwanted and unloved will be greatly reduced, and you will start to believe me when I tell you that not having a boyfriend does not have anything to do with not being lovable.

The fact is, there are "dry spells" and "flood times" in everybody's life when it comes to boyfriends. You may be going through a prolonged dry spell right now. In a little while, however, you may find a boyfriend—and not only that, you may then meet other guys who are also attracted to you. "Why couldn't I have met them before, when I didn't have a boyfriend?" you'll wonder. Why is it always feast or famine? At the same time that you find yourself enjoying a sudden surplus of admirers, one of your friends may have no boyfriend and feel as miserable as you did when you didn't have one. See how it works! But you probably won't spend too much time feeling sorry for your friend, just as your friends don't spend much time worrying about you. It's human nature. We play down other people's pain because we do not feel it ourselves, and we magnify our own discomfort because we are living it.

Even if it seems to you that nothing like this ever happens to any of your friends, only to you, rest assured that it will. There's not a girl in the world who won't at some time be without a boyfriend—and be miserable about it. You have plenty of company—even if, unfortunately for you, none of your friends happens to be in that situation now. So don't assume that something is wrong with you, just because you have the bad luck to be boyfriendless when none of your friends is. You're a victim of bad timing, not an unlovable creep.

176

None of these perfectly rational and sensible thoughts, however, can lessen the loneliness you feel when your friends are all so busy with their boyfriends that they neglect you. Yes, it's lonely at times like this, yes, it hurts not to be included in your friends' social life. Still, there are some advantages—believe it or not—to not having a boyfriend. I realize that it's not what you want, but, since it's the hand life has dealt you for the moment, you might enjoy hearing how other girls have made the best of it.

## ADVANTAGES TO *NOT* HAVING A BOYFRIEND

When I asked girls to tell me some of the advantages of not having a boyfriend, they had plenty to say.

You can have male friends and talk to other guys without stress. It's fun to enjoy your freedom. Also, if you meet a new guy you're interested in, you don't have to worry about what you're going to do about your boyfriend.

*Atasha, 16*

You don't have to sit at home and wait on his phone call, or fear that he's mad at you or something is wrong.

*Lorraine, 15*

I made new friends and hung out with my cousins. It was great not having to report to anyone.

*Tami, 18*

You get to go out on dates with many different guys. You can go to parties and meet all sorts of people.

*Megan, 17*

You pay more attention to school, and read more and you have a better relationship with your mom.

*Jeanie, 16*

When you don't have a boyfriend, you get into yourself—you look at your life and what changes you want to make. You can also get into your hobbies and sports.

*Andrea, 17*

You don't have to worry about him cheating on you or getting caught cheating on him.

*Simone, 14*

Basically, when you don't have a boyfriend, you're freer. And when you're free, of course there is less stress. There's nobody—besides your parents, of course—to account to. (Bad enough you have to account to them.) There are none of the pressures that are built in to any male/female relationship—no worry about what he might be doing behind your back, and no need to hide what you're doing; no arguments, no anxiety about what it means when he doesn't call, no demands on your time; no dread of breaking up; nobody to please but yourself.

In addition, you can do so many other things with your new free time. It's at moments like this that you realize just how much time your boyfriend was taking up, time that you could have been spending on interests that he may not have shared, such as playing a musical instrument, working on the school paper, taking scuba diving or ballet lessons, or running track, or time that you needed to get higher grades in school, study for the SATs, read interesting books, or write in your journal. You might also use the time to work at a part-time job and make money, or participate in extracurricular activities that would look good on college applications (and maybe help you meet new guys).

Once you realize how valuable your time is, you'll want to think twice about whom you spend it with in the future. In short, you may become more selective in choosing your next boyfriend. If you're going to sacrifice your precious time for him, he'd better be worth it, you may find yourself thinking.

Very often when we're in a relationship, we not only don't take the time to do the kinds of things I've just suggested, but we get so involved in the ups and downs of the moment that we don't take time to consider our long-range goals. What direction do we want our lives to take, what professional aspirations do we have, how do we feel about our relationships with family and friends and so on? When you find yourself free and alone, instead of looking at it as a punishment, realize that it's an opportunity to grow, explore, reflect on, and pursue your goals.

## WHAT IS YOUR GOAL AND WOULD YOU GIVE IT UP FOR YOUR BOYFRIEND?

We touched on this question in Chapter 9, when we discussed guys not worth keeping—specifically those *guys who stop girls* from pursuing their goals. Here we'll talk about *girls who stop themselves* from pursuing their own goals because they believe their boyfriend is more important than anything they might want to do. I asked girls: "What is your goal and would you give up your goal for a boyfriend?" Before you read on, answer the question yourself. The girls' answers vary.

I want to be a teacher and marry a businessman. I would give up my goal for him because love makes me do extremely stupid things.

*Cyndi, 17*

I want to be an Olympic gold-medal winner in the Women's 3000. I'm already the best in my state. But I would give it all up for love. I'd do anything that pleases him—if I felt he was the one I wanted to marry, and if I thought he was worth the pain.

*Jessica, 15*

I want to be a lawyer. I wouldn't give it up for a guy because you end up hurting yourself if the relationship goes sour.

*Linda, 16*

179

I want to become a successful psychologist and author, marry a great guy, and have beautiful children. You will have many loves in your life, but ultimate satisfaction comes from reaching your dream. If you miss your mark, it doesn't matter how perfect your boyfriend is, you'll never be truly happy. You will miss your whole purpose for being created in the first place. Not a good idea! Find your love after you do what must be done.

*Marthe, 16*

I want to be a successful entrepreneur. If he really loves me, he will be willing to adapt his goals to mine. He should be helping me to reach mine.

*Kim, 16*

I want to be a nurse and make lots of money. It's my career. He wouldn't give up his for me. I'm not going to ruin my life for a guy.

*Jen, 13*

Being a successful interior decorator is my goal, and I wouldn't give it up for a guy, because if we broke up (even after we were married) I would never forgive myself for throwing away my life. I can find a boyfriend and keep my goal at the same time.

*Liz, 16*

I want to be a pediatrician. But if I listen to my boyfriend, I'll end up on welfare. No one is going to destroy my future.

*Stephanie, 17*

My mother made that mistake. I think you can have both a man and a career—if you're patient. But if I had to choose one or the other, I'd choose my goal.

*Helen, 14*

I want to be a model. If a guy said "Give it up. I'll support you," I'd tell him to go to hell. Why should I give him power over my life?

*Edith, 16*

Cyndi is right about it being "stupid" to give up her goal for love, and Jessica is correct—whether she knows it or not—about the fact that there will be a lot of pain if she's foolish enough to relinquish her goal of being an Olympic gold medalist for a guy. She'll hate the guy later and blame him for the loss, but worse than that, she'll blame herself, because in her heart, she'll know that it was her own fault. Before anyone is even trying to force her to stop "going for the gold," she's already gearing up to do just that for the right guy. There's no reason to abandon your goal for a guy. In fact, as Kim points out, he should be helping you reach it. Once he sees you're serious about it, he may. If, however, you show yourself only too ready to abandon it for him, don't be surprised if he takes you up on the offer. Why shouldn't he? How nice for him that you're willing to serve him and his goals and forget your own. In the long run, however, he may not only come to take you for granted, but may even lose interest in you because you'll have so little life of your own. As for you, you may be one of those women always dreaming about what she could have been if only . . . Now's the time to start making the if-only come true.

When I think of all the would-have-been doctors, lawyers, scientists, writers, dancers, musicians, actresses, athletes, and so on, who "gave it up for him," it makes me so angry I could jump right out of this book and shout "Don't do it. Please don't do it."

Anyway, you're lucky. These days, it's not really expected that you give up your goal for a man. In the fifties I had to fight the tide, when I insisted on going to college and pursuing a career, while most of my girlfriends wanted only to get married and begin having babies the moment they graduated high school. Why didn't I follow in their path? I didn't because I was lucky enough to have parents who helped me to see that I had a choice. I saw the trap and I refused to fall into it.

What's it going to be? Will you try to realize your full potential, or will you sell yourself short and regret it later?

Keep in mind that any guy who makes you choose between him and your potential is looking out for his interests alone. What kind of a husband would he make anyway?

## LIVING WITHOUT A BOYFRIEND WHEN YOU'RE STILL IN LOVE: OR, BREAKING UP IS HARD TO DO

All well and good. You know how important it is to put your goals before a boyfriend, and you realize that there are advantages to not having a boyfriend, but what do you do if you've been going out with a guy for a long time and you're still deeply in love when he announces that he wants to break up? How do you cope with the beginning stages of the breakup? How do you get over him? How do you even live from one day to the next when you feel as if your heart is breaking? I asked girls to give advice on this subject. They say:

Feel the pain, write sad poems, listen to blues songs—you'll get over it eventually.

*Sunny, 17*

Love pain hurts, but it doesn't kill. Believe it or not, life goes on and you can learn from your mistakes.

*Kara, 15*

Think about the bad things he did and count your blessings. Work overtime and make money to buy pretty clothes so you can meet better guys.

*Sara, 16*

Throw away all his pictures and forget that idiot. People have happy second marriages, so why can't they have happy second relationships?

*Lydia, 16*

You lived the years before you met him, so you can live without him now. There are lots more guys out there, and you'll be surprised, the next guy can be better than the

182

one before. How do you know he won't be? You didn't know how good the one you're missing now would be when you first met him, did you?

*Willa, 16*

Love finds you when you least expect it. Get excited about the future. In the meantime, talk it out with your family and friends.

*Millie, 18*

Your first love is always the most painful. You think you will die if it breaks up, but you get over it and the next love is better. Take it from me. I know.

*Irene, 19*

Put it in God's hands. Maybe it was for the best, and it was too early to settle down with one guy.

*Dolores, 15*

It isn't the end of the world, though it seems that way. Time passes and soon you wonder what you saw in him. Time heals all wounds.

*Marthe, 16*

Breaking up with someone you still love, especially if you've been going out with that person a long time, is very painful. It would be foolish for me to advise you to pretend the pain isn't there, to put on a happy face and to smile, smile, smile. Sunny and Kara are right in advising you to let yourself feel the pain. I remember to this day when the love of my life broke up with me, at the age of fourteen. All I wanted to do was listen to jazz-blues. Somehow it would comfort me as I got into the depths of the wailing instruments and lamenting lyrics. I also found comfort in tear-jerking country and western songs, and I wrote lengthy poems about how my heart was breaking. In addition, I talked to my friends, repeating the story again and again, until I felt better.

Since those teen years, I've survived other very painful breakups. I've learned to channel my anger and frustration energy into positive areas, such as karate, running, working on various projects, and so on. You can do the same, and in the end, you'll have something tangible to show for it, rather than mere frustration, and that in itself will help you to feel better. For example, if you do the twelve-minute total-body workout every day (see bibliography), in a few months your body will improve so much that every time you pass a mirror you'll smile with pride. You'll say to yourself "I'm glad I didn't spend that time crying in my room. Now look at me." And your improved physique will give you more confidence when it comes to meeting new guys. In addition, exercise causes a natural high as endorphines are released to your brain. You'll be in a better mood after you exercise —whether you follow my workout or do any other form of exercise, from swimming to jogging, biking to ballet.

Sometimes when you break up, you think of all the wonderful times you had and you picture yourself doomed to suffer forever without them. You remember the way he held you, the way you danced together, the way he complimented you, the sweet things he said—and you torture yourself by dangling those wonderful memories before your eyes.

Instead of doing that, why not take Sara's advice and think of the negative things that used to happen in the relationship—the times he kept you waiting by the phone and never called, the times he insulted you, the arguments you had, the times he was insensitive, and so on? Think of the frustration and anger you experienced in the relationship, and you may start realizing how lucky you are to be out of it.

You're probably very angry with him and wish you could cut him out of your mind. Well, you can cut him out of your life symbolically, if you have a picture of the two of you together—with a pair of scissors. It may help you to feel better if you cut him out of any picture he's in with you and cut to shreds any picture you have of him. The physical act of cutting can help you to reinforce your determination to make a clean break from him and to look forward to the bright new future. It reminds me of the old song: "I'm Gonna Wash That Man Right Out of My Hair."

As much as you may not think so at the moment, you *can* go on without him. You functioned quite well before you ever met him, didn't you? And you will meet another boyfriend—perhaps when you least expect to. I can prove it. Did you know you would meet and fall in love with this last boyfriend? What notice did you get? None, of course. It was a complete surprise. So it will be with the next.

If this was your first love, you probably don't need me to tell you that the first one is the most painful one to lose. Why? You can't imagine ever feeling that way again. In fact, you don't believe you will. It reminds me of tasting ice cream. Suppose the only ice cream you ever tried was vanilla, and you loved it. Then the vanilla was canceled, and the manufacturers of ice cream said it would never be made again, but they would make other, even more delicious flavors in the near future. You would probably not be very comforted, and would keep thinking about that vanilla— until you tasted strawberry, chocolate, pistachio, butter pecan, or peach. Then you'd *know* better.

So it is with love. Each love seems the best ever, until you find the next one, which makes the old one seem uninteresting. For those of you who have had more than one love in the past, I'll bet you can already testify to this by looking back at some of your old boyfriends and comparing them to later boyfriends. Time and maturity make all the difference. Soon, believe it or not, you'll look back at this one, too, and wonder what all the fuss was about. Think back to your grade-school crushes. Isn't there someone you were mad about then whom you think about now and say "Yuk. What did I see in him?"

## ARE GIRLS HAPPIER WITH A BOYFRIEND OR WITHOUT A BOYFRIEND?

There are three groups: those who are happier with a boyfriend, those who are happier without a boyfriend, and, the most well balanced of all, those who are happy either way.

## Happier with a Boyfriend

I'm happier with a boyfriend because I have someone to laugh with and love and tell my problems to.

*Sylvia, 15*

I need a boyfriend to share my feelings with and to have fun with and take me out.

*Dorine, 18*

I have someone to look forward to seeing and I know I am not alone in the world.

*Diane, 16*

## Happier Without a Boyfriend

I'm happier without one because I don't have anyone nagging me or telling me to stay home. I can flirt more.

*Rebecca, 14*

There's no heartache and no worries at all. I don't have time for the pain.

*Lillian, 17*

I have more time for my friends and for myself.

*Trudy, 16*

## Happy with a Boyfriend or Without a Boyfriend

I'm really neutral because sometimes I wish I had more time to myself, to explore, but sometimes you need someone to hug and kiss and tell you he cares for you.

*Nancy, 15*

When I do have one I'm content. Yet I miss the fun of wondering who I will meet tomorrow.

*Andrea, 17*

Both ways. I share different kinds of likes. I enjoy the good things about a boyfriend, but don't like paying the price of being tied down. Then again I enjoy the good things about being free, but don't like the loneliness I feel at times. But I'm basically happy either way.

*Dina, 14*

Nothing is all glory or all pain. Having a boyfriend has its advantages, and being without one also has its advantages. What's really important is that you realize that you can be happy with or without a guy in your life. If you can learn to take advantage of both situations, you'll find yourself enjoying life a lot more.

If you have a boyfriend and things are going well, enjoy it. If he becomes a burden and he's not worth keeping, drop him and enjoy your freedom. If you meet another guy and he fits into your life and enhances it, great. If a guy breaks up with you, realize that it's probably meant to be and that another love will come along. In the meantime, realize that the more time you have to spend toward advancing your talents, interest, sports, and hobbies, the better. Any guy who gets in the way is trouble. (The good ones, however, will encourage you.)

When you were a baby, you couldn't survive alone, but now you can. You always have yourself. You have a will of your own and you can do whatever you want to do with your life—you don't need a boyfriend to do it. Do I hear any "amens" out there?

# BIBLIOGRAPHY

**Other Books for Teens by Joyce Vedral**

*I Dare You* (New York: Ballantine Books, 1983). A "how to win friends and influence people" for teenagers. Motivates teens to overcome obstacles and achieve goals and shows them how to use psychology in dealing with teachers, friends, bosses, and so on in order to make things run more smoothly.

*My Parents Are Driving Me Crazy* (New York: Ballantine Books, 1986). Gives teenagers insight into the workings of the adult, specifically "parent," mind. Helps teens to become more loving, compassionate, and understanding of parents. Teens who have read the book say that it has totally changed their relationship with their parents.

*My Teenager Is Driving Me Crazy* (New York: Ballantine Books, 1989). Get this book for your parents if you want them to understand what goes through your mind when you do certain outrageous things, such as come home late, tell them how to dress and behave, borrow their things without asking, hang out with the "wrong crowd," neglect important chores, and so on. Tells parents what teenagers really worry about. Helps parents to learn how to listen to teenagers without interrupting with a lecture and how to talk to their teenagers so that teenagers will listen. Lets parents know that all of their hard work is not in vain and that many of their values are really getting through to teenagers, even though they may not find out until the teen is an adult. Gives specific examples of when a teen was about to do "the wrong thing" and stopped himself because his parents' words came to mind.

*I Can't Take It Any More* (New York: Ballantine Books, 1987). Shows teens how to deal with anger, rage, hate, fear, rejection, and other emotions that could potentially destroy their lives. Gives them specific ways to take these emotions and use them to achieve goals rather than allowing them to turn inward against themselves. This is *the suicide prevention guide,* and many young adults have written that the words from this book have come back to them to encourage them when they were having suicidal thoughts.

*The Opposite Sex Is Driving Me Crazy* (New York: Ballantine Books, 1988). Helps teenagers to understand why the opposite sex behaves the way it does. The book is divided into halves: Girls answer favorite questions posed by boys in one half, and boys answer typical questions asked by girls in the other. Topics such as jealousy and cheating, sex, spending time and money on each other, turn-ons and turn-offs, and standard lectures parents give their sons and daughters (and how they differ) are covered. Teens are helped to realize that they are not "weird" or "rejects" and are given ways to deal with even the most cruel behavior of the opposite sex.

*The Twelve-Minute Total-Body Workout* (New York: Warner Books, 1989). An intense exercise program requiring only one pair of three-pound dumbbells and utilizing the "dynamic tension" of the martial arts in combination with bodybuilding movements. Each of the nine body parts—chest, shoulders, triceps, buttocks, thighs, abdominals, back, biceps, and calves—is exercised two to three times a week. Helps teenagers (and adults, too, for that matter) to attain a firm, well-defined body. Includes a nutritious diet that helps teens to lose excess body fat without sacrificing good nutrition.

You may order any of the above books by calling 1-800-733-3000.

Joyce Vedral is also author and co-author of several other fitness and diet books.

*Now or Never*
*Supercut: Nutrition for the Ultimate Physique*
*Hard Bodies* with Gladys Portugues
*The Hard Bodies Express Workout* with Gladys Portugues
*Perfect Parts* with Rachel McLish
*Cameo Fitness* with Cameo Kneuer

# Index

192

193